LEGACY OF

VIRTUE

LEGACY OF
VIRTUE

A Devotional for Mothers

Amy Nappa &
Jody Brolsma

PROMISE
PRESS
An Imprint of Barbour Publishing

ISBN 1-57748-493-2

Legacy of Virtue: A Devotional for Mothers is another creative resource from the authors at Nappaland Communications Inc. To contact the authors, send e-mail to: nappaland@aol.com

Unless otherwise noted, Scripture quotations are from the Holy Bible, New International Version, copyright © 1973, 1978, 1984 by the International Bible Society.

Published by Promise Press, P.O. Box 719, Uhrichsville, OH 44683
http://www.barbourbooks.com

Member of the
Evangelical Christian
Publishers Association

Printed in the United States of America.

DEDICATION

To our mother, Winnie Wakefield,
who taught us compassion, hospitality,
and how to short-sheet a bed.

We love you!

CONTENTS

FOREWORD

Today I read through the devotions in *Legacy of Virtue: A Devotional for Mothers* and quite a few memories came back to me. As a mother of ten active and imaginative children, I could recall a lot of the same circumstances in my own life as those expertly written about in this book. How unique and helpful *Legacy of Virtue* will be to mothers as they raise their children according to the Word of God!

If you're a mother, it will be helpful because you'll find yourself mirrored in a number of these devotions. As we mothers reflect on this thought-provoking book, we'll learn several lessons.

For instance, we'll be encouraged to be more patient (in the devotion entitled "Cheerio Excuses and Moey Oh Decoders"). And, through the humor of the devotion entitled "Stick to It," we'll also be reminded of truth about motherhood. Specifically, we'll remember that although raising your children is definitely work—as is teaching your children discipline, love, and character—we mothers are granted an unspeakable joy that comes with watching our children grow and mature in Christian character.

As I read over these pages today, one thing they continually bring to my mind is how much fun I had with my children. Amidst all of the work involved in taking care of them, I always had fun with them. This is a truth that should never be lost on any mother. Your children need to enjoy you just as much as they honor and obey you.

In this book there are pages and pages of illustrations — both humorous and serious—that can help you in your bad times and encourage you in your good times. These are truths that mothers can return to over and over again, truths of enduring virtue from which we can be refreshed.

Most importantly of all, Amy Nappa and Jody Brolsma have based this book on the Word of God. Each chapter opens with a relevant Scripture from the Bible. It's been my experience over these past forty-five years of my own married life that God's Word is what takes you through each day.

I highly recommend *Legacy of Virtue* to all mothers seeking to know the truth and seeking to create a virtuous legacy for the children they call their own.

—DELORES "MOM" WINANS

THE INHERITANCE

The only thing that parents
can take to heaven is their children.
—Gigi Graham Tchividjian [1]

The wise inherit honor.
Proverbs 3:35

I wanted Mom's jewelry!"

"Well I wanted the dining-room set!"

"It's mine!"

"No, it's mine!"

It sounds like the bickering of young children, but in reality it's the fighting that often occurs between family members after a parent passes away. Everyone has heard stories of a sister who got to the house before the other siblings and cleaned out all the valuables or a brother who ransacked the safe-deposit box without the others knowing. Perhaps this has happened in your family.

Several years ago our parents made a list of all their valuables.

Grandmother's china.

A bed with an intricately carved headboard.

Mom's cedar chest.

A large mirror.

The items on Dad's workbench.

The list was several pages long.

Five copies of the list were prepared, one for each child in our family. We were to read through the list and write our names beside the item we wanted to inherit when our parents died. Then our parents would read over these lists and create a master list, designating who was to receive each item. We could make our requests, but the final decisions were theirs.

The purpose of the list was to make sure there would be no hurt feelings between the children. No fighting, no bitter tears, no regrets hardening in our hearts. Our parents wanted to pass on their belongings in a controlled, thoughtful manner.

We are a sentimental family. As we children read the lists we not only saw the item listed, we also recalled the memories attached to them.

Grandmother's china, which we had used at holidays and other very special occasions.

The intricately carved headboard had been crafted by a great-grandfather. . .and remember the great forts we made under that bed?

Mom's cedar chest held all the tiny crocheted dresses we girls wore as babies, plus lacy clothes and fine linens. The hours we could spend looking through it, saying, "Oh! Look at this!" and "Remember when Jill wore this?"

Turn the large mirror over and you'll find it had been signed by all the members of a church our parents once attended and where they were dearly loved. It was a going-away gift given before a move years and years ago.

Dad's workbench holds tools both old and shiny new. Think of all the toys he mended, the hope he restored as a bent bicycle handle was straightened, the gadgets he created, his hands holding these tools.

Our parents weren't passing on to us only their valuables. They were passing on their memories. Their love. Their legacy.

You will pass on more to your children than your belongings. You'll pass on to them the memories of time you've shared, the values you held, the virtues of your life.

What are those virtues? How are you passing them to your children right now? You don't need to die to give your children an inheritance. Let's begin right now.

Lord, help me to remember
the most valuable things I have
right now are my children.
Let them inherit from me virtuous hearts.

SPITTIN' IMAGES

She's got her Father's eyes.
—Gary Chapman[2]

Then God said,
"Let us make man in our image,
in our likeness."
Genesis 1:26

He's the spittin' image of his mother!"
Yes, it's true that Amy's son, Tony, has green eyes, exactly the same shade as Amy's. His hair color matches hers, their skin is the same tone, and their noses are remarkably alike.

But "*spittin'* image"? What do looks have to do with expectorating? What does this phrase mean?

According to the dictionary, this phrase means "a perfect likeness or counterpart."[3] We use this saying most often when referring to how much one family member looks like another. But its original meaning has nothing to do with spewing saliva, and it implies more than simply having Mom's great smile. Instead, it comes from the saying "spirit and image." This saying was passed on and heard with a lazy accent here and there, and eventually "spirit" was shortened into the slang "spit."

Ahh. Now this makes more sense. Tony is like Amy in image. His looks resemble hers. But the big question is, is he like her in spirit? We're getting deeper into who the mother and child truly are. Is Amy reflected through Tony's actions, through his personality, through his very being?

A child can be adopted and share no physical resemblance to his or her mother. But through years of living together and the familiarity that comes with time and relationship, this child can reflect the spirit of his or her adopted mother. The child can be like her in spirit.

We are sisters who do have a strong resemblance. In fact, Amy is thrilled when people ask if we're twins, as she's got seven years on Jody and loves to know people think she still looks young. Not long ago a kindergartner at our church stopped Amy and asked, "Is that one that looks like you here?" We reflect each other in our image. And although we are not personality doubles, we do have many common interests, views, and loves. We are alike in spirit.

Much of who we are was passed on to us by *our* parents. We are very much the image of our mother. And we are like her in spirit. We have her love of people, her mischievous sense of humor, her tender heart toward those who are hurting. And, we have to admit, we have her quick temper and are often moved to tears. Just like Mom. So when someone says to us, "You're just like your mother!" we take no offense. In fact, it's a compliment.

Do you look at your child and see yourself? Not merely

in physical attributes, but in spirit. Are you passing on what is truly most important to you? How wonderful to have someone who knows you and your child say, "He's just like his mother. Maybe he doesn't look like her, but he has the same virtuous heart."

> *Lord, let me see Your love*
> *pass through me and be reflected*
> *in the actions of my child.*

A VIRTUOUS WOMAN,
WHO CAN FIND?

As a mother,
I must faithfully, patiently, lovingly,
and happily do my part—
then quietly wait for
God to do His.
—Ruth Bell Graham[4]

Her children arise
and call her blessed.
Proverbs 31:28

We're getting ahead of ourselves if we decide we're going to leave a legacy of virtues to our children but never discuss what virtue is. The literal definition of virtue is moral excellence. We then take this further and outline specific virtues such as courage, perseverance, loyalty, and so on. These are character traits that must be learned—we're not just born with them.

Virtue is not something we have—it is what we are. For

example, we cannot physically give our children the virtue of courage. It's not a medal we can hang on them as the Wizard of Oz does with the Cowardly Lion. Instead, we teach our children to be courageous. We teach them to sleep in a dark room, to remove that tiny spider themselves, to walk through the doors on the first day of school. We teach them by our words and, even more importantly, our actions.

Of course, to teach these virtues, especially through our actions, we must be virtuous ourselves. What exactly is a virtuous woman? Perhaps you picture a nun wearing a dark habit, cloistered away from society, and eternally kneeling in prayer. Or a pious and reverent woman who always does the right thing, always has the right answer, and who's memorized the entire Bible—in the King James version no less.

Yes, these women probably are virtuous, but how can we ever live up to these ideals? In reality, we're soccer moms, businesswomen, and grandmothers with toddlers in tow. We have a diaper bag in one hand, a briefcase in the other. Children clamor about our legs while we discuss PTA meetings on the phone, stir dinner with one hand, and pull the dog off the table with the other. We're busy, our lives are hectic, we lose our tempers, cheat on our diets, and speak without thinking. What kind of virtuous legacy can we leave behind, much less live?

Relax. It's our guess that you're actually more virtuous than you know. For starters, work is a virtue, and we all know how hard mothers work! So you've got one there already!

Use this book to help you consider what virtues are already evident in your life and to challenge you to grow stronger in other virtues. Then finally, reflect on how you'll pass these virtues on as your legacy to your children. It's not too late to get started!

Gracious Lord, I will never be
as excellent as You are.
Yet help me to become more virtuous
and like You as I strive
to grow closer to You.

DRENCHED IN JOY

I don't want to go in the deep end.
—our youngest sister, Annette Wakefield,
upon viewing the ocean as a child

Shout for joy to the Lord, all the earth.
Psalm 100:1

Our mother loves the anticipation of planning a fun event, but she can often be a "spur of the moment" type of person as well. As Amy recalls, "Just before I began third grade we moved from Kentucky to southern California. Mom immediately had us out in the water, learning how to 'jump' the waves and coast along in the surf. But school began and our beach adventures were soon over for the year. Or so we thought.

"One day Mom picked us up from school. With five kids ranging in age from infant to eight, she had plenty to keep her busy. It's not like she needed any extra hassles in her day. But this day, she started along the road to home, then suddenly exclaimed, 'Let's go to the beach!'

"Did it matter that it was November and there was a bit

of a chill in the air? Did it matter that three of us were in school clothes? Did it matter that we had no towels in the car? Of course not! We all agreed with squeals of delight and shouts of affirmation. We were off.

"Within minutes we were at Huntington Beach. 'Roll up your pant legs,' Mom instructed. 'And don't get wet above your knees.'

"We were determined to obey. Until Joel just happened to splash Jill a bit too enthusiastically. Until Amy spied a shell just a bit farther into the water. And so it went until we were drenched at least to our waists or more. Mom waded along the edge of the surf with the two littlest ones, laughing and calling out to us.

"Finally it was time to go home. We were shivering with cold and covered with sand. Mom piled us into the car and we headed for home.

"Now, as an adult, I think how much hassle it must have been to later vacuum all that sand out of the car, to clean up after us as we trailed grime and seaweed into the house. I'd be saying, 'I'll never do that again!' But not Mom. We made several more out-of-season, no-towels-handy, I-just-got-a-great-idea trips to the beach or other locations over the years. The joy of it all must have been so immense to Mom that she just couldn't resist."

Are you resisting joy because it's a bit too much trouble? Forget all the extensive planning and jump into action the next time you think of something fun to do. Treat yourself to an afternoon matinee. "Accidentally" open the door of the ice cream parlor instead of the fabric shop. Skip out of the routine and into an outing that will leave a joyous memory in its wake. And watch out for Joel—he's still a bit too enthusi-astic in the surf.

Gracious Lord, nudge me
out of my routines
and into the joys of life.

MORE JOY THAN
YOU CAN IMAGINE

Does God have a sense of humor?
He must have if he made us.
—Jackie Gleason[5]

Your love has given me great joy and encouragement.
Philemon 1:7

Their lives started out terribly bleak.

As a baby, Rosie was only fed once a day and was forced to eat from a bowl on the floor, next to the dog.

Little Jesse's mother hit him with a skillet, then dropped him from a second-story window.

Sara's mother pushed her down a flight of stairs when Sara was only two.

Thirteen children just like Rosie, Jesse, and Sara began life with several strikes against them. Birth defects. Abusive parents. Malnutrition. Who ever would have believed that their lives would someday be filled with overwhelming joy and love? Sue and Dale Clem made that happen.

In the past twenty years, the Clems have adopted thirteen disabled children. Children that nobody wanted. Children who may have been doomed to a loveless existence, with no family to care for or about them. Yet in spite of the wheelchairs and medicine that are a part of daily life, the Clem household is filled with love and laughter.

"It's a lot of work, but there's more joy than you can imagine," says Sue. In fact, she'll acknowledge that a sense of humor is critical. "We're always clowning around."

Take, for instance, their twenty-one-year-old daughter, Teri, who has a fixation on bathing suits. Teri sleeps with twenty bathing suits every night and occasionally adorns her wheelchair with them. "The agency told us Teri was always going to be a vegetable, but we're still trying to figure out what kind she is," Sue laughs.

The Clems play, laugh, and love wholeheartedly. And as a result, they've brought extraordinary changes to the lives of thirteen children. "This is the girl they said could never show love," says Sue, holding Rosie close.[6]

What an amazing difference joy can make. In the Clem household, it brings healing every day. It sheds light into dark and hopeless lives. It gives strength to tackle overwhelming challenges. Happiness has nurtured hope and security. What difference can joy make in your home?

> *Gracious Father, fill my heart,*
> *my home, and my life with joy.*
> *Help me pass Your joy to others each day*
> *so that their lives may be changed forever.*

JOY IN THE MIDDLE

I've got the joy, joy, joy, joy down in my heart.
Down in my heart to stay.
—George W. Cooke[7]

I am greatly encouraged;
in all our troubles my joy knows no bounds.
2 Corinthians 7:4

ho do you think would be joyful?

   a. an Olympian basking in the exhilaration
      of a gold-medal finish
   b. a mother contentedly rocking her perfect
      newborn baby
   c. an actress accepting an Academy Award
      for her stellar performance
   d. a young woman with learning disabilities
      dealing with the day-to-day challenges
      of life
   e. all of the above

If you knew our sister Annette, you'd understand that the answer had to be "e." Annette was born with learning disabilities that affect her physically and mentally. At twenty-seven years of age, she functions at about a junior high level. Yet, if that was all you knew about Annette, you'd be missing the best part.

Annette's middle name is Joy, and no one in the world could have chosen a more fitting name. Indulge us for just a moment and let us tell you more about our sister.

She is a high school graduate.

She is a compassionate, caring friend. . .who loves to talk on the phone for hours!

She is a cheerful giver—always looking for an opportunity to take you out to lunch or treat you to frozen yogurt.

She is a diligent and gifted caregiver to children. (She's even learned sign language so that she can better communicate with handicapped kids!)

She is a trustworthy confidante.

She loves to laugh. . .and does it often.

Annette's life has been filled with challenges. Eye operations, speech therapy, special schools, hurtful words. Many people would be filled with bitterness and anger, shaking their fists at God. Yet Annette has overcome each obstacle with tenacity and, most of all, a joyful heart.

In the movie *The Sound of Music*, Julie Andrews (portraying Maria Von Trapp) has a wonderful quote. She says, "When God closes a door, He always opens a window." Annette's life could have been a closed door, but God "opened a window" by graciously pouring extra joy into His precious creation.

In the quiz you just took, did you notice something about the first three answers? The people were all joyful *depending upon their circumstances.* A first-place finish, a happy baby, a prestigious award. But a truly joyful heart finds happiness in any situation. Life itself is reason for delight.

Do you let your circumstances dictate your "joy quotient"? Is life a joyful journey for you? If people could choose a middle name that described you, what might that name be?

Father, help me put Your joy
in the middle of my life today.

SOMEONE TO WATCH OVER ME

If you make children happy now,
you will make them happy
twenty years hence by the memory of it.
—Kate Douglas Wiggins[8]

Again Jesus said,
"Simon son of John, do you truly love me?"
He answered, "Yes, Lord, you know that I love you."
Jesus said, "Take care of my sheep."
John 21:16

Donna Leonard has always hated Mother's Day. Unable to have children herself, she always felt cheated on Mother's Day. At church the pastor always called out, "Let's have all the mothers stand so we can applaud them!" Every restaurant she stopped at those spring Sundays found mothers being given flowers, free desserts, or other gifts of honor. For Donna, however, there was nothing. Eventually it began to hurt too much, and she stayed home each Mother's Day to avoid all the fuss.

Much of what we write in this book is directed toward

mothers. But every woman leaves a legacy—mother or not. In fact, one of the women we think has left the greatest legacy of virtue in recent history is Mother Teresa—who never was a mother in the biological sense. Through her works of love, she inspired thousands of people to live more joyful, giving, and godly lives.

Our friend Donna, along with her husband, Stan, never had biological children, but literally hundreds of college students consider this couple their spiritual parents. Donna and Stan welcomed lonely kids into their home and hearts. They had students over for barbecues. They delivered irises from their incredible garden to anyone in need of encouragement. They gave godly counsel and direction as it was needed. They were parents in love, if not in reality.

Two of our sisters are not yet mothers. Yet they leave a legacy of virtue as well. Jill has been involved with kids in a ministry to poor inner-city children. She has given these kids her time, plenty of hugs, and even her telephone number. Annette works as a caretaker for children with cerebral palsy. As we mentioned earlier, Annette is challenged in her own abilities, yet she learned sign language to better communicate with some of her charges. How special they must feel to know someone cares enough to learn how to talk to them. And both of these sisters spend countless hours with their nephews and nieces. The kids watch their beloved aunts and learn virtue through them as well.

Even if you do have children, it's not just your own flesh and blood to whom you leave your legacy. There are children watching you everywhere! Your children's friends are watching you as they come into your home to play or spend the night. They notice if you are impatient about a loud stereo or if you show compassion over their skinned knees. Our friend Rene remembers how kind the mother of one of her high school boyfriends was to her when Rene would stop by their home. "It was her example that led me to the Lord," Rene shares.

Kids at church are keeping an eye on you. One mother told Amy she'd caught her preschool-aged son wandering around his house calling out, "Show starts in five minutes! Puppet show in five minutes!" When asked what he was doing, he answered, "I'm being Amy!" It seems he'd seen her announcing an upcoming puppet show during a church party a few weeks before! This young boy was imitating the actions he'd seen just once. We simply cannot know how much of an impact our repeated actions have on children around us!

Think about the children with whom you come into contact. The kids you see when you volunteer at your child's school. The children you care for in your home. The car pool gang. Your kids' friends. The neighborhood children. The teenager who baby-sits for you. Your grandkids. They're all learning from your example.

So even if you're not a mother, you've got a lot to give. (You probably have more patience to give as a starter!) The joy and love in your heart might be just what's needed to make a big difference in the life of a child. What a legacy!

> *Gracious Lord, thank You for giving me*
> *the opportunity to touch so many lives.*
> *Help me to remember that each child is*
> *precious in Your sight,*
> *whether it's my child or someone else's.*

SURPRISE!

My mother is made of clay and play.
—anonymous child[9]

But may the righteous be glad
and rejoice before God;
may they be happy and joyful.
Psalm 68:3

As we were growing up, our mother gave us great advice. "Keep your elbows off the table."

"Send thank-you notes to your grandmother."

"Be sure to wear black when you're toilet-papering a house."

Yes, our mother has quite a reputation as a prankster. One of Jody's greatest memories of Mom is when Jody finally got to go along on a t.p. adventure late at night. You know what "t.p.ing" is—"decorating" a friend's yard with rolls (and rolls and rolls) of toilet paper. And when it comes to toilet-papering a yard, Mom is the best! Along with teaching us our manners, reminding us to send thank-you notes to Grandma, and helping us with homework, Mom also instructed us in the fine "art" of practical jokes. She's the world champion at just about any harmless prank that keeps people on their toes. (Our poor father, to name one!)

Here's just a sampling of the best pranks she's passed on to us. Try them on your family. (They'll think you're nuts, but they'll love the anticipation!)

- Sprinkle pepper in the toothpaste. (Dad thought his toothpaste had mildewed!) Be sure to have a spare tube on hand so no one blames you for that new cavity!
- Never underestimate the power of simple surprise. Jump out from behind a door and say "Boo!" (This is Jody's husband's first memory of Mom. And, yes, Jody *was* embarrassed!)
- Loosely stitch the legs of someone's under-wear together. (This assumes that the person is a close family member.) People will turn the item inside out and backward before they figure out what you've done!
- Bake a roll of toilet paper into an angel food cake. Be sure to invite a family member to slice the cake when it's time to eat. The look on his or her face will be priceless.
- Stretch a sheet of plastic wrap over the toilet seat. Talk about a surprise!
- Loosely stitch the towels to the towel

rack—just enough to make them "stick" when tugged at. (But be sure your towel racks are firmly attached to the wall.)

- Use a fresh bar of soap when soaping windows. Soap that's left out of the package tends to be hard and won't "write" as well.

Mom's "surprises" were never harmful or mean. They were fun reminders of her creativity and love for life. And what better way to go through life than with your eyes wide open, ready for the next delightful surprise.

God, thank You
for the wonderful surprises
You sprinkle into my life.
Give me the joy and creativity
to surprise someone today.

JOYFUL NOISES

I love to laugh!
—Uncle Albert in the movie *Mary Poppins* [10]

Our mouths were filled with laughter,
our tongues with songs of joy.
Psalm 126:2

Nothing warms the heart like laughter. Everyone crowds around a baby trying to get this newborn child to smile, coo, and giggle. We hear our children laughing and just the sound makes us break into a smile. People look forward to inviting humorous friends to parties because their stories amuse us so. Comedies, even of the goofiest kind, are always popular movies.

At Amy's house there's an ongoing competition of who's the funniest. Says Amy, "I think I'm pretty funny, but my husband and son always groan at my jokes. I think they just don't get them!"

Statistics show that adults laugh an average of fifteen

times a day, while children laugh an average of four hundred times daily. That's not hard to believe. Stop by any playground or park and you'll hear laughter over every other sound. Kids chasing—and laughing. Kids swinging—and laughing. Kids slipping down the slides —and laughing. Why are adults such bores? A crowd of grown-ups will have a few laughs to punctuate the murmurs of conversation, but we've got some serious catching up to do!

Maybe one reason kids laugh more is they know better jokes. Eighty percent of people claim they have a good sense of humor, but 96 percent of these people can't tell a joke. Can you tell one right now? Quick! Can't remember one? We think you'd better head to the bookstore or library and grab a copy of the latest joke book.

One thing we women have going for us in the laughter department is that we already out-laugh men—by 127 percent! This seems evident when you listen to laugh tracks on television shows. There's always a woman shrieking or guffawing in laughter. And this is probably how groups of women got the reputation for sounding "like a bunch of cackling hens." Maybe it's like Amy's situation at home—women just "get" jokes more often than men!

Here's a great reason to laugh: One hundred laughs is the aerobic equivalent of ten minutes on a rowing machine![11] So if we turn on *I Love Lucy* every day, we can eat as much chocolate as we want! This is the best dieting plan we've ever heard!

And there have been plenty of studies that claim laughter has medicinal value. Some people claim they laughed their cancer away, laughed their stomach muscles to strength again, and, well, laughed in the face of death.

What makes you laugh? When was the last time you laughed good and long? Who can really tickle your funny bone? What makes your kids laugh? How often do you laugh together?

Have you ever considered that when the Bible instructs us to "make a joyful noise," that joyful noise just might be laughter?

Father of Joy, let me find
plenty of reasons to laugh today—
to throw my head back,
open my mouth,
and make a loud and joyful noise.

A JOYFUL EXAMPLE

Always be a first-rate version of yourself,
instead of a second-rate version of somebody else.
—Judy Garland[12]

In everything set them an example
by doing what is good.
Titus 2:7

She's won eight Grammy Awards, nine Dove Awards, and five Stellar Awards, just to start the list. She's had two platinum albums (selling over a million copies), three gold (selling over 500,000), and three number one radio hits. Her list of professional achievements seems endless. Yet when asked about her greatest accomplishments, Christian singer CeCe Winans puts motherhood at the top of the list. Here's what she has to say:

"Just to see them grow is an incredible experience to me. First of all, to carry them—what an experience! A great experience, to feel something alive in you and then to birth it out. You just see God in every stage. It's such a spiritual experience along with being such a great natural experience. But to see their faces. To see them grow into young adults. To maturity. To see them laugh. To be there with them when they're crying. To be able to make them feel better. You know, it's a wonderful feeling as a mom. To even get worn out. I don't know why that's a wonderful feeling, but it is. To be worn out by your children is great to me. You know you're running around for them all day long. It's like 'I don't even have a life of my own. I do everything for you all.' But it's a joy, you know, to be able to nourish somebody."

CeCe says the best advice she received about motherhood came from her own mother, Mom Winans. That advice is, "To be a good example in front of your kids and to love your kids unconditionally. I think my parents loved us in a way that we knew no matter what we did, they would be there. That's the advice I got from them, saw from them, and received from them. And even to this day, I know no matter what I've done, it's not too bad to tell them. And that's what I want to establish with my children. That's the type of relationship I want to have with them because I know it's not easy all the time. But I want them to know that we're there for them no matter what they're going through and that we're going to love them just the same. I think that's great advice."

We can only imagine how hectic life was for Mom Winans raising ten children. And we can only imagine how hectic life is for her daughter, CeCe, as she balances raising her two children with her incredible career. Yet in spite of the pressures and all the busyness, these women desire to be godly examples to their children. How does Cece do it?

40

"God. I put Him first. It's a constant balancing, though. It's not something that you just set and you keep it there and it works all the time. But having the Lord first is definitely the thing that you set. It's a constant thing. You always have to say, 'Am I doing too much? Am I spending enough time with the kids? Am I spending enough time with my husband? Is this really important? Do I have to do this? God, is this where you want me to go?' You learn that you have to eliminate all the unnecessary running. You know? So having God first is definitely the answer. I believe family is definitely supposed to be right after Him and everything else comes after that. That has always been my motto and that's what I've stuck with through the years and it's worked. It's something I've had to fight for because people will not put your family first; they will put the business thing first and the appearances first and I've had to demand that. And now they know. They know what I stand for and what I believe in, so it works."

No matter what your profession, life is hectic. And no matter what your profession, your children are watching you. What are your priorities? What comes first in your life? What place does God have? Where does family fit in? As the Winans women have said, "Our lives are our example to our children." What kind of example are you setting?

Lord, let me look to You for guidance
as my children watch me.
Let me point them to You as the greatest example of all.

BUT WHY?

No pain, no palm;
no thorns, no throne;
no gall, no glory;
no cross, no crown.
—William Penn [13]

Whatever you do, work at it with all your heart,
as working for the Lord, not for men.
Colossians 3:23

There is a world record for everything.

In 1993, a Peruvian man was declared the champion joke-teller when he told 345 consecutive jokes—all in one hour. [14]

Two people in England set the world record for escalator riding in 1989, when they spent five days on an escalator in a London store. They went up and down the escalator 7,032 times.

Ashrita Furman completed 390 games of hopscotch in twenty-four hours to set the world record for hopscotch. Furman should be considered "Mr. Guinness," seeing as he holds fifty-seven world records for feats such as juggling, pogo-stick juggling, milk-bottle balancing, and long-distance somersaulting.[15]

Imagine the hours of practice these folks put into achieving these records! ("Mom, I'm going out to practice my backward unicycling now.") The amazing thing about setting any kind of world record is that it takes tremendous tenacity and discipline. (Come on, hopping *10,000 meters* in a peanut sack?) And after the juggling, hopping, or escalator riding, someone has his or her name in the record book. But that's all. It's not to say that world records are bad, they're just a lot of effort and work for no reason.

Most of us exercise self-discipline for specific reasons. You want to stay thin, so you avoid those double-chocolate-with-fudge-frosting brownies at the church potluck. You want a better job, so you take that night class and stay up late, working on papers and studying. You don't want your child to have a mouth like a sailor, so you stifle your cries when your tender feet walk across a sea of Legos on the kitchen floor. Those actions all require self-discipline, for clear and noble reasons.

However, one area of our lives that requires self-discipline is often forgotten. Our relationship with God. God calls us to pray and read His Word faithfully. We don't know about you, but for us, that takes a lot of discipline! Pressing schedules, deadlines, family members, and busy days crowd out that time with God. It takes determination and discipline to stick with it! So why the effort and work and struggle to make that time for prayer and Scripture reading? Why bother? Because God loves you.

If a man can balance sixty-two glasses on his chin, certainly you can set aside time each day to get to know God. Remember, God didn't mind sacrificing something valuable for you.

Precious Savior, thank You
for sending Your Son to die for me.
I want so much to know You more
and spend time with You.
Forgive me for the times when I brush You aside
for other "more important," foolish things.
I love and treasure You.

QUOTABLE QUOTES

Wait a minute! Wait a minute!
You ain't heard nothin' yet!
—Al Jolson in *The Jazz Singer*,
the first "talkie"

With the tongue we praise our Lord and Father,
and with it we curse men,
who have been made in God's likeness.
James 3:9

Quiz time! See if you can correctly name the movie and actor that matches each of these quotes:

1. "Toto, I have a feeling we're not in Kansas anymore."
2. "I'll be back."
3. "Life is like a box of chocolates; you never know what you're gonna get."
4. "Hold your breath, make a wish, count to three."

5. "Well, as somebody always said, 'If you can't say anything nice about somebody, come sit by me.' "

6. "Zuzu's petals. There they are!"

7. "Here's looking at you, kid."

8. "If we bring a little joy into your humdrum lives, it makes us feel as though our hard work ain't been in vain for nothin'. Bless you all."

9. "After all, tomorrow is another day!"

10. "Love means never having to say you're sorry."

Okay, most of these were pretty easy, and if you check the answers at the end, we'll bet you got most of them right. In fact, even if you've never seen some of these movies, it's likely you've heard these quotes from one source or another. And certainly you have your own favorite movie quotes. One of our favorites is from *Little Women*: "I could never love anyone as I love my sisters."

So what is it that makes these words so memorable? If you cry at movies, perhaps an utterance pulled at your heartstrings and started you sobbing. For the romantics, it might have been a dreamy line you wish you could hear whispered in your own ear. Or the delivery of an expression may have tickled your funny bone and caused you to burst out laughing. Whatever it was, you remember the words. They are imprinted in your mind.

There may be other words imprinted in your mind.

Words you wish you'd never heard. Words you wish you'd never said. Unkind words. Angry words. Words of gossip. Words that have torn another down or broken a heart. Your tongue may be as sharp as a two-edged sword.

In the Bible, James compares the tongue to a bit that can guide an animal, the small rudder that steers a large ship, the tiny spark that turns a forest to ashes. He then laments that we have managed to tame or control "animals, birds, reptiles, and creatures of the sea," yet we cannot control our tongues.

A virtuous woman has the self-discipline to control her tongue. When a neighbor fails, she doesn't pick up the phone to spread the word—even under the veiled gossip of "I just want you to know so you can be praying. . . ." When her child loudly asks, "Why is that man in a wheelchair?" she never hisses, "Shut up you idiot!" When her husband forgets to wash the dishes, at no time are her comments bitter.

Consider the movie quotes you so easily remember. What quotes will others remember coming from your mouth? Will it be words of anger? Or words of love?

"You're the best!"

"I love you!"

"It's okay. We can work it out."

"I'm sorry."

"I'm proud of you!"

Hopefully the next time there's a contest to see who can identify the source of *these* quotes, you'll be the winner because you'll know every kind word has come from your mouth. And every person to whom you've spoken these words will be a winner, too.

Lord God, cause my heart to well up with
words of love toward others.
Control my lips and tongue and
bring forth only words honoring to You.

ANSWERS:

1. Judy Garland in *The Wizard of Oz*
2. Arnold Schwarzenegger in *The Terminator*
3. Tom Hanks in *Forrest Gump*
4. Gene Wilder in *Willy Wonka and the Chocolate Factory*
5. Olympia Dukakis in *Steel Magnolias*
6. Jimmy Stewart in *It's a Wonderful Life*
7. Humphrey Bogart in *Casablanca*
8. Jean Hagen in *Singin' in the Rain*
9. Clark Gable in *Gone With the Wind*
10. Ryan O'Neal in *Love Story*

A SILENT DEBATE

Self-control,
another word for restraint,
is honored by the Lord
as the "anchor virtue"
on His relay team
that runs life's race
for His glory.
—Charles R. Swindoll[16]

Like a city whose walls
are broken down
is a man who lacks self-control.
Proverbs 25:28

After listening to the first thirty seconds of the book, I knew I should turn off the tape and turn on some music," relates Jody. "It was a suspenseful mystery that grabbed me right from the beginning. . .and terrified me just as soon! I try to listen to books on tape at the gym, to make the time on the Nordic Track go faster. Well, this book certainly got my heart pounding! And my mind racing. And my imagination going into overdrive. Even though I knew that the story would give me nightmares, I kept telling myself, 'As soon as I'm done exercising, I'll turn it off. Really. I mean it. I'll just finish this side of the tape.'

"At 2 A.M. I lay in bed with the covers pulled up to my chin, eyes wide open. I really had to go to the bathroom, but there wasn't any way I was getting out of bed. All I could think about was the creepy psycho in the book. Why did I have to listen to that book?"

Self-control is kind of like a gravy boat. Sure, you've got it, but you don't ever use it. We battle with our conscience, bargaining for one more minute of sleep, one more hour of television, one more piece of pie, one more new sweater, or one more page of a scary book. We know we shouldn't, but we find the most imaginative (and illogical) ways to justify our actions and push self-control out the window. More often than not, self-control often loses the inner debate.

There's a line from an old children's song Jody remembers that defines self-control this way: "Self-control is just controlling yourself. It's listening to your heart and doing what is smart." What a simple guideline to pass on to our children today. (And one that we should try to remember ourselves!) When the inner battle wages, do what is smart.

As you try to pass on the virtue of self-control, keep this thought in mind. Let your kids bolster *your* self-control. Tell them the areas in which you struggle. They'll offer wonderful incentives and reminders when you're tempted—

sometimes you'll honestly believe that they can hear your inner debate.

> *Heavenly Father, I want to develop*
> *the fruit of self-control.*
> *I want You to win that inner debate,*
> *guiding me to do what is smart.*
> *I pray that my children*
> *will also turn to You for direction*
> *when self-control is hard to find.*

DISCIPLINE OF THE HEART

I've learned that
after being on a diet for two weeks,
all I lose is fourteen days.
—sixty-year-old person[17]

I can do everything through him
who gives me strength.
Philippians 4:13

On her wedding day, Shari Hayes was a size 20. Her new husband loved her, and friends who had gathered on this special day declared she looked radiant. But Shari felt differently inside.

"I didn't like myself," she shares. "I knew God loved me no matter what, but He wanted to work in my life and make me grow."

So shortly after her wedding day and with the support of her husband, Dan, Shari began one of the ultimate tests of self-control. A diet.

Yes, we've all been on diets. Some with success, most

without. Shari had tried other diets, too, but this time she was determined to succeed. So instead of starving herself with celery sticks and grapefruit juice or counting every calorie, Shari made big changes in her life.

First, of course, was eating. "I had to change my eating habits and learn how to eat right." Next, she disciplined herself in exercise. "Exercise can be hard," she admits. "I tried to exercise with a friend for accountability, fun, and encouragement." She sought encouragement from the Scriptures by hanging verses about her home to help her say "no" to temptation. And her loving husband added incentive by offering her a dollar for every pound lost. "We didn't have a lot of money, but a little helped."

Sounds so simple, but we all know from experience that it wasn't. The self-control required for dieting is long-term, not just turning down dessert once a week. Shari remembers, "The hardest part was that it took a long time. One and a half years, slow and steady. It was a long haul, but it paid off." Of course Shari got discouraged at times, but instead of indulging in chocolate cake, she treated herself to a new scarf or a video. And the compliments of friends who noticed her slimmer body did wonders to keep her on course as well.

As a result of the discipline of those long months, Shari lost eighty pounds. She went from a size 20 to a size 8. Dan gave her the eighty dollars and she went out to spend it all on new, smaller clothes. And, even more amazing, Shari has kept that weight off for more than ten years. This truly was a permanent change of lifestyle for her.

Is thinness a virtue? No. However, discipline and self-control are, and Shari certainly has demonstrated these in her life. She doesn't hide away her wedding pictures. Instead, she's proud to tell others of how God helped her reach a difficult goal. She is teaching her daughters a healthful lifestyle and, most importantly, is teaching them to follow God.

Shari encourages us in her own words:

"Seek the Lord when you know God wants you to do something. I wanted to please Him most of all. My motivation was to make the Lord proud and ask for His strength in my weakness. He wants to give us victory through anything that is pleasing to Him. Don't give up. Keep going toward your goal even if you feel it's too far away."

Loving God,
You have the strength to move mountains.
Give me the strength to move
away from the refrigerator.

STICK TO IT!

In ev'ry job that must be done
there is an element of fun.
You find the fun and snap!
The job's a game.
—Mary Poppins[18]

My heart took delight in all my work,
and this was the reward for all my labor.
Ecclesiastes 2:10

Bubble gum is big business. If you don't believe us, just follow along as we take an imaginary tour of a bubble gum factory. . . .

One of the first steps in creating bubble gum is deciding upon the flavor. True, "bubble gum" itself is a flavor (ever had a bubble-gum flavored snow cone?). But this gooey stuff also comes in flavors such as kiwi, blue raspberry, lemon-lime, and grape. In fact, one flavor could actually be a combination of up to twenty ingredients!

You enter the flavor-tasting labs to begin the process.

The lights in the room are all red, so it appears that each piece of gum is the same color. You won't get to choose your favorite by color. And who is joining you on this adventure? Kids, of course! After all, they spend about half a billion dollars on bubble gum each year. So the room is full of muscle-mouthed kids, their mouths jammed with globules of gum. You join in the masticating and decide upon your favorite flavors.

It turns out that strawberry and watermelon are top flavor favorites with the chomping champs. Yet gum researchers (can you imagine telling someone this is your job?) are always looking for new flavor combinations to capture the fancy of chewers. And besides the flavor, you have to rate the sweetness, stickiness, texture, and bubble-making ability of each piece you chew. Are your jaws tired yet?

After being tested by up to five hundred kids (and you!), a new flavor is finally decided upon and sent on to production. Here you enter a sanitary facility where everyone is clad in white lab coats and hairnets. After all, who wants hair in their gum? The first stop is at a small weighing station. With a sigh of relief you realize they don't want to weigh you, but the huge slabs of gum base. You learn that although these large, tan-colored chunks were once made from a rubbery natural material called "chicle," they're now created from artificial ingredients.

You move along to large vats where the slabs of gum base are melted into a gooey, syrupy consistency. Here they're mixed with sugar and the colorings and flavors all those testers gave the thumbs-up on, then stirred, tumbled, and finally squeezed into five hundred-foot-long ropes of gum. It's cooled, cut, packaged, and sent on its way to the stores.

All this work for a chunk of gum that will be chewed for a few minutes then find its way to the bottom of your shoe or your child's hair. (By the way, experts say the best way to remove gum from clothes is by freezing it with ice cubes and then chipping it off.) [19]

We know you care a lot about the children entrusted to you. Often the greatest expression of love is through work. Making special meals, washing clothes, driving here and there and back again, even disciplining your child can be work. Yet it's still a way to show your love. After all, aren't your kids worth more than a stick of gum?

Heavenly Father, put a smile on my face
as I go about my work today,
and help me to avoid getting "stuck"
on problems that steal joy from my life.

CHEERIO EXCUSES AND MOEY OH DE-CODERS

Raising children is as difficult as
nailing poached eggs to a tree.
—Unknown[20]

A patient man has great understanding.
Proverbs 14:29

"Dinnertime at our house has become a language lesson for my husband, Erik, and me," explains Jody. With a toddler, Brianna, trying her best to join in the conversation, our dialogue often goes like this:

> Brianna: Moey oh's.
> Jody: You want some *Cheerios*?
> Brianna: No. Moey oh's.
> Erik: I think she's asking for more of *those*. . . the
>   biscuits. (*points to the biscuits*) Is this what
>   you want?

Brianna: No. Moey oh's.

Jody: Oh, I know. She wants me to wipe her *nose*. Is your nose runny?

Brianna: No! No! Moey oh's.

Erik: Sweetheart, we don't know what you want. Now drink your juice and I'll get you some more spaghetti.

Brianna: Moey oh's.

(The light goes on.)

Jody: Spaghetti. . .oh's! Oh, she wants more SpaghettiOs!

Some nights it's like being on a game show—except no one wins a new car for guessing that Brianna wants to read *Pat the Bunny* again.

According to the Zandl Group, a New York–based marketing consulting firm, Jody and Erik's job won't get easier. Here's some of the slang they say is current among twelve- to twenty-four-year-olds:

"Bout it out" means "I'm up for it"

"True dat" means "That's right"

"Get my grub on" means "Eat"

"Cheerio excuses" means "Go around and around"[21]

Whether you're trying to interpret what they're saying or doing, understanding your kids can be a challenge. In Jody's case, Brianna is trying to piece together her language and communication skills. So it wouldn't be fair if Jody gave up and simply said, "Sorry, kid. I don't understand you. You're on your own." Instead, she has to work at each word, searching for understanding. Of course, that can be a lot of effort, but it's worth it. Brianna gets fed, changed, played with. . .her needs are met.

All relationships take work. Webster's defines work as "sustained physical or mental effort to overcome obstacles and achieve an objective or result."[22] What is your objective in your relationship with your child? Showing love? Being a friend? Showing him or her a Christ-like heart? Whatever the objective, it *will* take effort to achieve. It may be mental effort —trying to understand what your teenager is talking about, reasoning with your fifth-grader, or following along while your preschooler tells a story. It may be physical effort—not weeping when you see your daughter's room, biting your tongue when your son talks back to you, or simply standing your ground.

Relationships take work. It may be slow, frustrating, and sometimes downright painful. But it will always be 100 percent worth it.

Patient Lord, give me the patience
and understanding to work at
my relationship with my children.
Thank You for working on
my relationship with You.
I'm glad You never give up on me.

HUMBLE BEGINNINGS

Success in life comes not from
holding a good hand,
but in playing a poor hand well.
—Dennis Waitley and Rem L. Witt[23]

Blessed are you who weep now,
for you will laugh.
Luke 6:21

Many of today's most popular pastimes and playthings had humble beginnings. Some of them were even born from mistakes or failures. Consider the following:

During World War II, a spring popped from the engine of a navy ship. Richard James, the ship's engineer, told his wife Betty about it. Together, the two worked with the concept, coiling steel ribbon in a unique fashion. The result—it's Slinky, it's Slinky, for fun it's a wonderful toy!

The Frisbie Bakery in Connecticut didn't seem extraordinary. Their pies were popular on college campuses—but not necessarily for the taste. College students discovered that they could make the metal pie plates zip through the air with a mere flick of the wrist. Students would call out "frisbie" to warn others of the flying object. Thus, the Frisbee was born!

In the winter of 1891, a frazzled teacher was looking for an outlet for energetic students, cooped up inside during the long winter months. By using a peach basket and a soccer ball, the innovative teacher invented one of the most popular pastimes today—basketball.

Scientists goofed when searching for a substitute for rubber in 1945. The result of their experiment was a bouncy goo that didn't appear to be good for anything. But Peter Hodgson didn't see it as a mistake. He made a fortune packaging the bouncy material in plastic eggs as Silly Putty.[24]

A tired teacher, creative college students, an innovative engineer, a silly scientist—they all have something in common. They didn't give up. They turned everyday items upside down. They saw the ordinary as extraordinary. They all went the extra mile to make something marvelous from something mundane.

Face it, our lives are filled with common, ordinary things. And we make an awful lot of mistakes. (Remember last night's hamburger. . .er, "surprise"?) But that doesn't mean our lives need to be dull or mundane. It means that our lives are full of possibilities! If we have the "stick-to-itiveness" to work a little harder, we can turn seemingly broken things upside down. Take our "failures" and bounce them around a little. Leave *"what is"* in the dust and pursue *"what could be."* Go the extra mile, even when it seems ridiculous. Just think what your efforts might produce!

A woman told Jody about a family vacation that seemed

to bomb. The kids were whining. She and her husband were at odds. And to top it all off, they'd tried a shortcut and gotten lost. "We were ready to turn around and go home. . .if only we could find the way!" Finally, they pulled over and let everyone get out to stretch. As the kids explored the woods, she and her husband looked closer at the map and realized that they weren't far from a campground that featured a beautiful waterfall and stream. It wasn't where they'd planned to go, but it *was* just a few miles ahead. So they took a chance, stuck it out, and went for it. "It was the greatest, most memorable vacation we'd ever had. What started out as a failure turned out to be a wonderful surprise."

Loving Father, thank You for filling
my life with wonderful surprises.
Give me the wisdom to turn to You,
so You can turn my mundane into marvelous.

CHEERS FOR CHORES

Whistle while you work.
—Snow White[25]

If a man will not work,
he shall not eat.
2 Thessalonians 3:10

It's late in the afternoon and we're almost there. It was a fun camping trip, but now we're all tired, dirty, and ready to be home. Our old station wagon groans at the weight of the overloaded camper it pulls toward our driveway, and we all groan at the thought of unloading this same camper.

"Remember kids. . ." Dad starts off cheerfully.

"We know!" we indignantly interrupt.

What do we know? The Rule. No one goes to the bathroom until the car and camper are unpacked. With five kids and a dad who is reluctant to stop at every gas station along the road, you can be sure the chore is always completed in lightning speed.

When we were kids we often heard, "If you don't work,

you don't eat." This was our parents' reminder to us that everyone had to share some of the workload in our home. Of course, this saying, a variation of 2 Thessalonians 3:10, didn't always motivate us to action. So our parents devised creative methods such as "The Rule" to spur us on to action.

Perhaps you've invented your own methods to motivate your kids to get their work done. No dinner until chores are completed. No television until homework is done. Or a sticker is earned every time the beds are made. Yet despite all our creativity, it's still often a chore to get kids to do their chores!

Along the way, we've learned an important tip in getting kids to do their work: Do your own work with a cheerful attitude.

In reality, it can be hard to smile while saying, "I'm off to fold the laundry!" or to keep the sarcasm out of your voice as you utter, "I love my job!" But the way we approach work goes beyond ourselves and the task at hand. Others are affected.

One of us had a coworker who was always negative about every aspect of her job. Complain, gripe, protest. That's all one could hear coming from her desk. Not only did it make working near her unpleasant, but her attitude began to sink into the hearts of others and fester. Soon others were whining about their paychecks, lamenting the hours they put in, snarling about the boss.

Think about how this same scenario plays out in your home. You hate doing the dishes—do you think your kids are going to be jumping with joy when you ask them to help out? You grumble and slam doors every day as you leave for work—and you wonder why your kids have similar attitudes when you ask them to pitch in around the house. What goes around comes around. . . .

Your attitude about work will be reflected in your children, "Rule" or not. And speaking of The Rule, now we're grown and both have bathrooms near our offices. Even worse, we have refrigerators nearby. *Now* how are we going to get any work done?

Dear Lord, lighten my attitude
as You lighten my burdens.

EXCUSES, EXCUSES

It's Laura's fault; she broke the plate!
I tried to stop her!
She said she had to demonstrate her apple chopper!
The apple chopper worked just great
but chopped right through your bowling plate!
—Junior Asparagus from *VeggieTales*[26]

Then the Lord God said to the woman,
"What is this you have done?"
The woman said, "The serpent deceived me, and I ate."
Genesis 3:13

Have you ever read the warning labels on products in your home? You might be in danger! Before you move another muscle, here are some we think you should consider:

- Do not use as an ice cream topping—
  warning on a hair-coloring kit
- Warning! For indoor or outdoor use only!—
  from a package of Christmas lights

- Caution! The contents of this bottle should not be fed to fish—*on a bottle of dog shampoo*
- Do not use while sleeping—*label on a blow-dryer*
- Not to be used as a personal flotation device—*printed on 8-by-10-inch inflatable picture frame*
- This cape does not enable you to actually fly—*on the cape to a child's Halloween costume*
- Please remove before driving—*from a cardboard windshield shade*
- Do not drive cars in ocean—*small print on a car commercial that showed a car in the ocean*
- Not dishwasher safe—*on a remote control*[27]

We get a lot of laughs from these outrageous warnings. Who would think to toss a tiny picture frame to a drowning person or to feed their fish dog shampoo?

What's not so funny about this is that attorneys warn manufacturers that they must include labels like these on their products. Why? Because if they don't, and someone does try to drive their car with a cardboard windshield shade in place, and that person has an accident, they just might sue the person who made the shade saying, "You didn't say not to!"

We've become such a society of victims. Just like Eve pointing her finger at the serpent, we do not want to take responsibility for any of our actions. This begins from the time we're children pointing the finger saying, "He made me do it!" or "It's her fault, not mine!" One child we know looked at his graded test paper and said, "I know I wrote the correct answer, on my test. The teacher must have changed it to the wrong answer, then marked it." These attitudes then continue to the time that we're adults looking for someone to sue because we weren't warned that coffee is hot and will burn us if we spill it.

Most likely, you're not to the extreme of suing someone because your car won't drive in the ocean or you thought hair coloring foam would taste great on a sundae. Instead, you're cranky because your boss yelled at you. You head home and growl at your children before they even dare get into your way. It's not your fault—you've had a bad day. Or instead of admitting you have a problem with temptation, you blame being overweight on your husband, who keeps a carton of ice cream in the freezer. If he didn't like banana splits, you'd be thin.

We've got to stop passing the buck and take responsibility for our own actions. Things do happen that are beyond our control. Yet most of our problems are the results of our choices. We have to say, "These are the choices I've made, and I will accept the consequences." Or, better yet, make new choices and reap the rewards.

Dear Lord, thank You for giving me
the opportunity to make choices in my life.
Yet let me remember You will hold me
accountable for my choices as well.
Give me wisdom to make the best choices of all.

OPEN ARMS

Once like a leaf in the wind
Lookin' for a friend—Where could you turn?
You spoke the words of a prayer
And you found him there
Arms open wide—love in His eyes.
—Wayne Watson[28]

Defend the cause of the weak and fatherless;
maintain the rights of the poor and oppressed.
Psalm 82:3

It was the worst possible thing you could imagine for three children.

Their father had fallen from a scaffolding and died just four months ago. Now their mother was dead from the effects of her alcoholism.

The will specified that the children would go to an aunt's home. Unfortunately, the aunt was less than receptive. After two weeks with the children, she decided that they were too rambunctious and she couldn't handle the responsibility.

Now the children were homeless.

"I remember feeling so alone and frightened and wondering *Who would ever love me?*" recalls Leonard.

Then a hero stepped forward. Their oldest sister, Marion, only twenty-four and managing two toddlers of her own, took in her siblings. Not only did she take them in, she welcomed them with open and loving arms.

The responsibility was staggering. The little family was already having trouble making ends meet as it was. To take on three additional children would be a monumental task. But Marion was determined. "I couldn't bear to see those poor kids . . .never feeling safe or like they had a real home. . . . That was not something I could allow to happen. You take care of your family."[29] And so they made it work. The result? A warm home filled with laughter and treasured memories. A big family in which brothers, sisters, aunts, uncles, nieces, and nephews played and lived together. And incredible respect and admiration for a woman who took charge, even in the face of adversity.

In the Book of Proverbs, the author writes about "a wife of noble character." Proverbs 31:28 begins, "Her children arise and call her blessed. . . ." Marion's "children" have this to say:

"My sister Marion saved us. She's the biggest hero I have ever known."

"She treated every one of us as the most important person in the world."

"I think it was awesome of my mom and dad to take the others in, and we're all still really close today."

Marion didn't learn responsibility from her mother. But the lesson she's passed on to her children and siblings is clear.

The impression that she's made on them will last a lifetime. Her loving, responsible actions will impact a family for generations to come.

Heavenly Father, give me the eyes
to see the needs of my family.
Give me the courage
to step forward and act
when it would be easier to stand still.

LIFE IN THE MINORS

Don't Sweat the Small Stuff. . .
and It's All Small Stuff
—title of book by Dr. Richard Carlson

Consider how the lilies grow.
They do not labor or spin. Yet I tell you,
not even Solomon in all his splendor
was dressed like one of these.
Luke 12:27

The park is huge, especially in the eyes of a five-year-old. Ten baseball fields are marked within this grassy expanse. Around the perimeters coaches are dragging bags of equipment as they try to determine which of the red-and-white-shirted kids belong to their teams. T-ball season has begun.

When Amy's son, Tony, was five, he joined this T-ball league and began learning the rules. Hit the ball. Run. Catch the ball. Throw it to the pitcher. Pretty basic.

After a few weeks of these simple drills, it was time to actually play a game. Tony's turn came and he stepped up to the plate. He whacked the ball off its stand and watched it roll across the field.

"Run!" the coach yelled. And Tony did.

His little legs churned as he headed for first.

Another player stopped the ball and picked it up, then waited for someone to tell her what to do with it.

"Run!" yelled Amy. So Tony moved on, heading for second.

By now the ball had been thrown in the general direction of the pitcher, but had ended up near first base.

"Run!" yelled all the parents as Tony touched second, then third. He was nearer, nearer, nearer to home plate. He made it!

And all the adults began to laugh. Tony had run to the home plate on the next playing field over, bumping into a confused batter. But to Tony it didn't matter. He shrugged and trotted on back to his own team. He was playing a game and playing hard. The fact that he'd crossed from one field onto another was a minor detail.

Next it came time to man the outfield. There Tony liked to put his glove over his face and look at the sky through the tiny holes between the laces. It was boring out there, and the clouds looked pretty cool that way. Who cares if you forget what's going on and a ball rolls right over your shoes while you're goofing off? Details!

Remember life when the details didn't matter? Before you knew all the rules? Or before you made all the rules?

Consider this household scene: every lamp-shade and upholstered item covered in plastic. Family members are

74

required to eat snacks over a trash can to avoid dropping crumbs. The towels in the bathroom are only for display—the ones you're allowed to use are hidden under the sink. This is the home of a guy one of us dated in high school. Needless to say, the kids in this house got out as soon as they could and found other homes in which they could relax and "let down their hair."

Many women tell us life in their homes is stressful—their kids make their lives a headache. Too many glasses getting broken, too much milk getting spilled, too few beds are made, and so on. But these women are creating their own stresses, their own rules, their own unhappy homes.

Did God make you responsible for seeing that every glass in your home remains unbroken for the rest of your life? Did God put you in charge of bed springs, warning, "I'll be back in ten years and if a spring has been bent due to any jumping on this bed, I'll know"? Did God say He'd hold you liable for every bed that went unmade, every crumb on your carpet, every grass stain on your laundry?

Of course not! These are the minor details of life. However, God did entrust you with a child. Maybe several children. They are your responsibility. Not just their outer appearance, but their hearts. So instead of building a home that passes the white-glove test, you should be building a home filled with God's love, joy, and peace.

Life is huge. Skip the details.

Lord, You have given us much
in the gift of our children.
Let us take this responsibility joyously.

POINTING FINGERS

The buck stops here.
—Harry S Truman[30]

For God will bring every deed into judgment,
 including every hidden thing,
whether it is good or evil.
Ecclesiastes 12:14

Jody's eleven-year-old niece, Dena, has a penchant for getting into mischief. (Just ask her mother about the time Dena put the cat in the dryer.) Dena's most recent adventure happened at a neighbor's house, where she and a friend were playing in the basement. Dena had heard that if you mixed baking soda and vinegar together, there would be a "cool" chemical reaction. So the girls mixed an entire box of baking soda and an entire bottle of vinegar together in a coffee can, then snapped the lid on tightly. Soon, the can rocked back and forth. (Pretty neat, huh?) Then it began to shake. (Uh-oh.) With a pop, the lid launched itself at the ceiling, and a volcano of white foam spewed into the air. The walls, floor, and furniture were soon spotted with white.

But the damage didn't end there. It turns out that the mixture was somewhat caustic, eating through furniture and even cement. When confronted with the damage, Dena pleaded innocently, "It wasn't my fault. I just *thought* of the experiment. I didn't actually mix the two together!"

Where do kids learn the fine art of evading responsibility? Don't worry, we adults model it perfectly. Read on:

When debts began piling up, a Virginia chemist turned to a rather unconventional means of earning extra cash. He began manufacturing methamphetamines in a university lab. When his actions came to light, the chemist used a "Blame Dan Rather" defense. He claimed that Dan Rather had explained how to make speed on his television program, *48 Hours.* Thus, it must be Dan Rather's fault that the chemist was drawn into the illegal activity. (This dense defense failed miserably in court.[31])

It seems as if it's human nature to pass the buck. In fact, the flowers in the Garden of Eden hardly had a chance to bloom before Adam and Eve were pointing fingers at each other.

Adam: I didn't do it, God. It was her—that woman you put here! Eating the forbidden fruit was her big idea. I didn't even want to do it. She made me do it.

Eve: Me? I'm not responsible! It was that mean old snake that told me to do it. I told him we'd get in trouble, but NOOO! He said it would be okay. He's the one you should hold responsible!

And the sin was passed on and on and on. It didn't really stop until Jesus, God's holy and blameless Son, took full responsibility for *our* wrongdoing. In a sense, He said, "The buck stops here." "It is finished."

Taking responsibility for our actions is tough. It hurts. It requires sacrifice and humility. It goes against our human nature. But it makes a lasting (and often eternal) impact.

Gracious Lord, I know I sin
and fall so short of Your glory.
Thank You for sending Your Son
to bear the blame.
Give me the strength and courage
to stand responsible for my actions.

THE FIGHT OF YOUR LIFE

My mommy always told me to do what's right!
To wash behind my ears and try to be polite.
Ya' see, she loves me so!
—Junior Asparagus from *VeggieTales*[32]

May the Lord direct your hearts
into God's love and Christ's perseverance.
2 Thessalonians 3:5

Turning off the warm spray of the shower, Dana Goodge was ready to begin the day. But instead of hearing the normal sounds of the morning, she was startled by screams coming from outside her apartment.

The thirty-three-year-old woman rushed from her home, looking for the source of the screams, and came across a scene from a nightmare. Two large dogs were attacking a child.

Dana raced for the little girl and picked her up. The dogs, a Rottweiler mix and a German shepherd mix, continued their attack on the girl, jumping and biting at her. Dana kicked and hit at the dogs, while desperately clinging to the girl and screaming for help.

The dogs were relentless. They pulled and tore at the girl, dragging her out of Dana's grasp and onto the ground again, where they continued their attack. With nothing else to use but her own body, Dana threw herself over the child trying again to deter the dogs. However, they continued their attack, now biting and tearing at Dana.

Finally two men began throwing rocks at the dogs. Dana saw the window of opportunity, kicked at the dogs again, and quickly carried the child to her apartment.

Both Dana Goodge and nine-year-old Selina Stevens survived this horrific ordeal, but only because of Dana's perseverance. She wouldn't let those dogs kill that child.[33]

We thank God that most children don't have to experience the terror Selina did. But our children are still exposed to forces with desires to knock them down and tear them to bits. The images of violence, hatred, and disrespect are glorified and made larger than life on television, in the movies, in the lyrics of popular music, and even in books targeted at children. These images are printed permanently in the minds of children, then left to grow.

A mother visiting our town recently bragged about how her three-year-old son loves to watch horror movies. The movies she named were R-rated—blood, gore, and mutilation movies. And this woman was proud that her son liked to watch them! We couldn't believe any mother would even admit to watching these movies herself, much less exposing the innocent eyes of her child to them. She obviously had no concern about protecting her child from the evils of the world.

It is so difficult to stand up for what is best for our children. It takes incredible perseverance to keep from buckling under the constant demands of "Why can't I go there? Why can't I watch this? Why can't I listen to that?" Sometimes it seems as if we're fighting off dogs as we stand firm to protect our children.

The virtue of perseverance isn't one your children will thank you for having any time soon. After all, they're under the impression that certain movies, bands, parties, groups of people, and so on, are incredibly cool. But years from now they'll be thankful you persevered in protecting them. They might even thank you!

Lord, give me discretion to know
what is best for my own mind
as well as the minds of my children.
Help me to choose my battles wisely
and to fight them with tenacity.

THE STRENGTH OF A BEAR

By perseverance
the snail reached the Ark.
—C. H. Spurgeon[34]

Consider it pure joy, my brothers,
whenever you face trials of many kinds,
because you know that the testing
of your faith develops perseverance.
James 1:2–3

Wanted: one brave person to enter the dens of hibernating black bears and perform scientific experiments. Life insurance highly recommended.

That may not be exactly how Hank Harlow got his job, but it does sum up his responsibilities. Hank and a team of scientists are studying hibernating bears to discover how bears maintain their muscle tone through five to seven months of deep sleep. In contrast, when people don't use their muscles, those muscles begin to lose strength almost immediately. In fact, cosmonauts who spend about a year on the space station Mir are so weak, they're usually *carried* from the aircraft. Living and working in a weightless environment, these men have no way to strengthen their muscles. Weakened from a year of inactivity, their muscles can't even support the weight of a human body.[35]

Most of us would love to live a "weightless" life—free from the pull of problems, the exercise of exhausting schedules, and the work of worry. There, we could float and drift through life's difficulties rather than bracing ourselves and straining to get through. But consider the result. Our spiritual muscle, the stuff that gives us the strength to manage each step, would deteriorate. We would be too weak to handle the slightest worry or complication.

The Bible tells us that trials prepare us for life. Just as an athlete goes through rigorous (and often painful) training, God allows difficulties in our lives to "train" us for the race of life. James 1:12 gives this perspective, "Blessed is the man who perseveres under trial, because when he has stood the test, he will receive the crown of life that God has promised to those who love him." The rewards for our determination are tremendous.

What is your attitude toward problems? Do your children see you fret and worry over difficulties? Are they learning that each dilemma is a major stumbling block. . .or a stepping stone? How can your approach to conflicts demonstrate a spirit of strength and perseverance rather than frustration and weakness?

What a wonderful gift you can give your children by helping them view their problems as pathways to victory. Watch them build their "spiritual muscles" as they work through difficulties. Pray with them, asking God for strength as they compete with adversity. Cheer them on as they train for the race of godly living. And be sure to celebrate each step along the way!

Loving Father, it's hard for me
to view problems as anything positive.
Give me the strength to grow in adversity
and the power to persevere.
Thank You for promising Your strength
when mine is gone.

FOSTERING COMPASSION

We hand folks over to God's mercy,
and show none ourselves.
—George Eliot [36]

The Lord is gracious and righteous;
our God is full of compassion.
Psalm 116:5

Moscow is the capital and largest city in Russia. Over eight million people live there.

There are only five foster families in all of Moscow.

Stop to think about that for a moment. Out of millions of families, only five are willing to take in children abandoned by their parents.

The reason? In Russia it's a great social stigma to adopt or take in a homeless child. The unwanted children, more than 30,000 of them each year, enter orphanages. There are currently more than 160,000 children in these institutions. Many were born to alcohol- or drug-addicted parents. Many suffer from physical or mental illnesses. The outlook is bleak.

When Irina Palezhayeva entered a Russian hospital years ago to give birth to her third child, she saw two babies abandoned there. Her heart was filled with compassion and she determined to adopt a child. Her husband, Amar Ayshakh, knew the plight of unwanted children firsthand as he'd been abandoned as a child himself. Amar's mother had married a widower who already had three children, and he certainly didn't want hers. Amar quickly agreed.

But the red tape was exhausting. Irina and Amar realized they would never be able to adopt a newborn. So they turned to foster care.

Instead of adopting a squirming newborn bundle, Irina and Amar opened their home to nine orphans, which when added to their five "home-grown" offspring, gave them fourteen children. Of the nine foster children, four are legally invalids. All are severely stunted physically, mentally, or emotionally. All require constant care.

Many stories of this nature would end up in *Reader's Digest* with a touching ending about how the children were changed by the love and dedication of their new parents and became astronauts, nuclear scientists, or, at least, college graduates. This is not one of those stories. Irina and Amar instead celebrate the steps of a child born without a right leg or the words they've coaxed from a child who is deaf. They express pride in two African children they've taught to speak Russian. They spend their days teaching reading and writing, as well as what's right and wrong.

"Well," you might interject, "at least we can have a warm feeling from knowing how loving and affectionate the children have become." Wrong again. Irina has taken these children to her heart simply because of her compassion for them. She doesn't know if they love her back. "It's not that they don't love us in particular," she says. "It's just that they have little capacity to love at all."[37]

This is truly the story of dedication. Of giving one's daily life. Of complete compassion.

Compassionate Father, open my eyes and arms
to those in need around me.
Help me be willing to give up a bit of my comfort
to increase the comfort of others.

LOVING LEFTOVERS

Oh, heartbeat of heaven,
I want you to be my own.
—Steven Curtis Chapman[38]

Show mercy and compassion to one another.
Zechariah 7:9

Helen ver Duin Palit has great taste. She attends chic parties with Hollywood celebrities and studio bigwigs. She rarely misses glitzy events such as the Oscars, the Emmys, or the Grammys. And you can count on finding her at the glamorous galas that follow movie premieres. But Helen isn't there to mingle with the latest celebrity headliners or dish about L.A.'s hottest stars. She's just there for the food.

Helen, founder of Angel Harvest, gathers the leftover delicacies from Hollywood's biggest bashes—morsels like fried rock shrimp, Norwegian salmon, tropical tiramisu, or macadamia biscotti—and delivers them to forty-two soup kitchens and homeless shelters in the Los Angeles area. Her New York organization, City Harvest, delivers more than 20,000 meals a day to local soup kitchens and shelters for the homeless, battered, or mentally ill. Through Helen's compassion, ingenuity, and determination, 120 cities in the U.S. and 70 cities overseas have established Harvest-style programs.

But according to Helen, she's just doing what has always been expected. "The message I got at home was to give back to the community," she says. Growing up, Helen saw her mother take part in several charities and even create a program to provide companions for senior citizens. Those seeds of compassion and charity have grown, nourishing thousands of people around the world each day.[39]

The people in your world hunger for compassion. They're starving for a listening ear, an outstretched hand, a shoulder to cry on, or an open heart. Jesus lived in a similar world—one that cried out for kindness. But Christ didn't just *tell* His followers to show mercy; He modeled tremendous compassion during His time on earth. Jesus reached out and touched the untouchable (Matthew 8:3), He fed those who were hungry (Mark 6:30–42), He welcomed outcasts (Luke 15:1–2), and He comforted the brokenhearted (John 11:17–44). As a result, Jesus' followers understood what it meant to show compassion. They gave to others in need (Acts 2:45), reached out to beggars (Acts 3:1–7), and encouraged those who were suffering (Acts 11:22–24).

What seeds are you planting? Do your children watch you ignore the outstretched hand on the street? Are they taking mental notes when you don't bother to volunteer at church? What message are you sending when you turn away and shrug, "I'm too busy"? What are they learning when your attitude shouts "I don't care"?

Take time to demonstrate kindness each day. Make compassion your passion! Plant one of these "seeds" each day:

- Give a hug to someone who is down.
- Offer an encouraging word rather than advice.
- Pray with your children for needs or worries they're struggling over.
- Help someone in need—carry groceries from the store, search for that runaway puppy, or offer to soothe a crying baby.
- Give your time—even a few minutes can make a difference.
- Listen.
- Forgive generously.
- Give what you can—a glass of cold water, a Band-Aid, a ride, or a telephone call.
- Remind people of Jesus' love for them.
- Remind people of your love for them.

Water your seeds with prayer and watch your children grow into compassionate, caring individuals. Their kindness can feed the souls of many.

Loving God, let me see others with Your eyes.
Help me touch them with Your hands.
Show me how to love them with Your heart today.

A PLATE OF FOOD

*The first thing Pooh did was to go
to the cupboard to see if he had
quite a small jar of honey left;
and he had, so he took it down.
"I'm giving this to Eeyore," he explained,
"as a present."*
—A. A. Milne[40]

*He upholds the cause of the oppressed
and gives food to the hungry.*
Psalm 146:7

He was ancient, ragged, dirty, and didn't like kids. But that didn't matter. We were scared to death of him anyway.

Mr. Larrabee lived across the dirt lane from us when we were young. The old farmhouse our parents had rented was far enough into the country that Mr. Larrabee was our only neighbor. While our house was filled with laughing, shouting children, his tiny hovel housed only him and his dog—his only friend on earth. Every day Mr. Larrabee and his dog would walk together, then retreat again into their shack.

"Stay on our side of the road," our parents cautioned. "Don't bother Mr. Larrabee." While we'd climbed the fences and stolen the strawberries of previous neighbors, we didn't need much of a warning to keep us away. There was too much to do, too many places to explore, too much fun to be had on our land. And why would we want to sit on the porch with such a crabby old man?

Mom and Dad saw beyond that grouchy facade. We'd only lived in the house a few weeks before Mom loaded food onto a plate and asked Dad to carry it over. She knew he wouldn't take anything from her, but might at least open the door to our father. She was right. The food was accepted, and Dad began to slowly be accepted as well.

Then one day Mr. Larrabee and his dog didn't come out for their daily walk. Dad went over to check on things and found Mr. Larrabee beside himself with grief. His truest friend, his dog, had died.

Now Mr. Larrabee wasn't the kind of guy you could put your arm around and comfort. It just wasn't his way. So Dad found another way. He noticed another farm down our lane with a litter of puppies running around their property. Dad put Mr. Larrabee into our car, drove down the dirt track, and a short time later came back with a smiling old man and two romping puppies.

That year at Christmas a huge stuffed dog in a cardboard train showed up for us children. It had come from Mr. Larrabee. He had gotten it for free when he took a subscription to the local newspaper. Now, Mr. Larrabee didn't read. Maybe he took the paper to aid him in house-training his dogs. Or maybe he took it so he'd have something to give us. We'll never know. What we do know is the compassion shown by our parents cracked his hardened heart.

Over the years we have seen our mother pile plates with food for our father to carry to many neighbors like Mr. Larrabee. Many hearts have been opened with this simple gesture. Maybe that's why we're doing the same thing ourselves. We hope our children will continue this legacy.

Heavenly Father, open my eyes
to see beyond the hardness in others.
Let my acts of compassion soften
these lives so Your love may grow.

LOVE BEYOND REASON

I'll be the shelter in your rain
Help you to find your smile again.
—sung by Amy Grant[41]

I will not leave you as orphans;
I will come to you.
John 14:18

Imagine that you are alone. Truly alone. For one reason or another, everything you have, everyone you love has been taken away. Perhaps it was drugs that destroyed your mother, causing her to leave. Or your parents were killed in a war. Maybe you were simply abandoned by a parent who couldn't handle one more responsibility.

What will you do? Where will you go? Who can you trust? Who will care for your basic needs? More importantly, who will love you?

On any given day, nearly half a million children who live in foster care will ask themselves such questions. These are children who've experienced tremendous physical and emotional pain, heartache, fear, and loneliness. They've been abandoned, orphaned, or pulled from homes that are unsafe. And they face so many questions.

Tess Thomas is trying to help answer some of those questions. A foster parent, Tess gave up a singing career to share her love with special-needs kids. Her home is often filled with six or seven youth, kids she calls "the hardest of the hardest." "We adults can take care of ourselves, but the needs of children have compelled me to look out for them." For Tess, looking out for her kids can be tough. She tells of staring down knife-toting, dueling teenagers, among other challenges. Yet, as a result of her faith and compassion, Tess brings tenderness and love to the lives of troubled teenagers.[42]

Rob and Rita Jurotich have their hands full, too. They adopted five children from an orphanage in Szklarska Poreda, Poland. The children—siblings ranging in ages from five to fourteen—had been abused by alcoholic parents, and the effects of such a home life have lingered. The Jurotiches have spent thousands of dollars on therapists, medicine, and tutors that their children require. In spite of the difficulties, Rob and Rita are committed to teaching their children what it means to be a family. "They're not used to being cared for, but they're learning."[43]

What would cause people like Tess, Rob, and Rita to give up a simple, carefree lifestyle and take on such incredible challenges? They have a heart for the lost. A desire for the lonely to know love. Their compassion rises above reason, goes beyond understanding.

Perhaps that's why compassionate acts—ones that

demonstrate illogical love—stand out in our minds. They're so selfless, so pure, that they just don't make sense! And after being on the receiving end of compassion, you just can't keep the news to yourself!

"I had a bad morning—nothing was going right—and to top it off, I missed the bus. Normally, that means I'd have to walk to school. But today Mom gave me a hug and said she'd be glad to give me a ride. The rest of my day was great!"

"I got into a fight at school and Mom had to come get me. I knew she was upset, but first she made sure I was okay. She gently bandaged my cuts and put ice on my bruises. While she sewed up my torn clothes, we talked about what happened."

"My mom took off work yesterday and we went swimming! I know she's really busy at work, but she spent the whole day with me! How cool!"

It may take some getting used to. It may take some creativity. And you can bet it'll take time. But it will blow your kids away!

Love beyond reason. Illogical love. Kinda makes sense, doesn't it?

> *God, thank You for loving me illogically.*
> *Open my eyes to new ways*
> *to demonstrate compassion*
> *to my children today.*

QUIET COMPASSION

Today it is fashionable to talk about the poor.
Unfortunately it is not fashionable to talk with them.
—Mother Teresa[44]

"Then the righteous will answer him,
'Lord, when did we see you hungry and feed you,
or thirsty and give you something to drink?
When did we see you a stranger and invite you in,
or needing clothes and clothe you?
When did we see you sick or in prison
and go to visit you?'
"The King will reply, 'I tell you the truth,
whatever you did for one of the least
of these brothers of mine, you did for me.'"
Matthew 25:37–40

We cannot think of any person in this century who demonstrated more compassion than a simple woman named Agnes. From the age of eighteen, Agnes devoted herself to serving God by loving those others considered unlovable, even untouchable. She scraped maggots from the wounds of diseased men and women. She bathed the bodies of filthy children while bathing their spirits in her gentle smile. She held the dying in her arms, offering the last words of love their ears would hear.

Agnes was humble, never asking anything for herself. To save money she would ride in the baggage racks of a train. She offered to work as a flight attendant so she could fly for free. And when she did fly, she refused to eat the food set before her. Instead she asked for a bag in which to save this food and asked for the scraps of the other passengers as well. Everything she had, everything she could find, everything she could beg for, she gave to the poor.

Agnes was never too vain to scrub floors or clean toilets. She was never too fearful to speak the truth, even if it offended those who heard it. Agnes was not too proud to ask for help.

For her compassion, Agnes received the Nobel Peace Prize. Because she was willing to obey God and love others, she was given one of the most prestigious awards in the world.

By now you've probably figured out that Agnes was better known to the world as Mother Teresa. This tiny woman in a white sari became famous because she had compassion and put love into action. Celebrities, politicians, and royalty all flocked to her side, each one wanting to learn something from her. Instead of basking in the glory, Mother Teresa asked these people to join her—to touch the sick, to wash the dirty, to hold the dying. And, amazingly, they did.[45]

It is incredible that one woman could become so lauded for doing what Christians were commanded to do thousands of years ago. Jesus told us to feed the hungry, welcome strangers, clothe the naked, and visit the sick and imprisoned. One woman is obedient and is a hero to the world, inspiring thousands to follow in her footsteps. Let us be obedient, too, and pray that our children will follow in our footsteps as well.

Merciful Father, let me show Your compassion
through the kindness of my words
and the gentleness of my touch.

LAWS OF LOVE

The best portion of a good man's life—
His little nameless, unremembered acts
Of kindness and of love.
—William Wordsworth[46]

Love your neighbor as yourself.
Matthew 22:39

Gearing up for a trip? You may want to keep these laws in mind before you leave:

- In Kentucky, it's illegal to marry the same man more than three times.
- It is illegal to set a mousetrap in California unless you hold a hunting license.
- Leave your rope at home if you're fishing in Tennessee. There, it's illegal to lasso a fish.
- In Natoma, Kansas, you'd be breaking the law if you threw a knife at a man in a striped suit.

- It's a misdemeanor to show movies that portray acts of felonious crime in Montana.
- In Kansas City, Missouri, children can buy shotguns, but not toy cap guns.
- Don't pucker up on a Sunday—if you live in Hartford, Connecticut, that is. There, it's illegal to kiss your wife on Sunday.
- In Minnesota, it is illegal to tease skunks.[47]

We don't concern ourselves with following laws like these. They don't make sense! They're silly and we wonder how in the world they ever came to be.

But there's another law that we are *commanded* to follow. In Matthew 22:36, an expert in the law asked Jesus, "Teacher, which is the greatest commandment in the Law?" In Matthew 22:37–39 Jesus gave the man more than he'd asked for, for Jesus told the *two* most important commandments. " 'Love the Lord your God with all your heart and with all your soul and with all your mind.'. . .And the second is like it: 'Love your neighbor as yourself.' "

In this law, Jesus commands us to be selfless. To put the needs of others equal to or above our own. Have you ever thought of selflessness as a law? Does it dictate your every action and decision? Or is it treated as one of the "silly" and "laughable" laws you just read?

Your children may view you as a law-abiding citizen, but do they see you following God's most important laws? Get out your "unselfish acts radar" today. Give yourself a mental ticket when you notice you're exceeding the "self speed limit." Pay your fines in loving, selfless acts that reflect God's presence in your life. Remember, it's the law.

Father, I want to follow Your laws today.
Help me find unique ways
to put the needs of others above my own.
May I be a law-abiding child of Yours.

QUITE A THING

He who gives to me teaches me to give.
—Dutch proverb[48]

But just as you excel in everything—in faith,
in speech, in knowledge, in complete earnestness
and in your love for us—
see that you also excel in this grace of giving.
2 Corinthians 8:7

A recent article in the *Denver Post* caught Jody's attention. It was about a man who willingly became a guerrilla hostage after trading places with an employee he had never met.[49] When Ed Leonard was abducted by Colombian guerrillas, his employer, Norbert Reinhart, began fervent attempts to free Leonard. He finally offered himself as a trade for his employee, and his offer was accepted. Now free, Leonard says, "I am very grateful. . . . I wanted to be out, but I didn't want anyone to take my place. It's quite a thing."

This incredible example of selflessness may make you shake your head and say, "Wow! I couldn't have done that.

What an amazing man!" You may not have the opportunity to give such an outward example of self-sacrifice, but you have smaller opportunities each day. Do any of the following sound familiar?

You had a million things to do today, when the school called to say that your daughter was sick. You put your needs on hold to care for your sick child.

It's Thanksgiving Day and everyone is watching football, playing games, working on puzzles, and eating. You, on the other hand, are scrubbing potatoes, stuffing a turkey, and making a pumpkin pie from scratch.

You labored for eighteen excruciating hours to have that baby. When the pastor announces the arrival on Sunday morning, your husband stands and holds up the baby like a trophy *he* won!

There's one piece of Grandma's fudge left. You've been waiting for a quiet moment when you could savor it. Just as you open the box, your son asks if there's a piece left for him. (Of course, you'll give it to him!)

For your birthday, a friend gave you gift certificates to your favorite department store. You've been planning to use the money to buy some new clothes for yourself (a rare luxury!). . . but somehow you end up spending it on back-to-school clothes for your kids.

Since September you hinted (as loudly as you could) that you really wanted a new pair of running shoes for Christmas. But when your husband gives you a new pair of slippers, you say, "How did you know? They're just what I wanted."

Although you could tell many more stories of times you

gave up your needs or wants for those of your family or friends, no one will ever hear them. You live out Matthew 6:3–4: "But when you give to the needy, do not let your left hand know what your right hand is doing, so that your giving may be in secret. Then your Father, who sees what is done in secret, will reward you." There won't be a headline "Woman Forfeits Bubble Bath to Work on Term Paper with Procrastinating Son." But God knows how much you give. He knows how much you give up. And His reward will be generous.

Gracious God, help me to put
the needs of others before mine.
Help me to be gracious and giving,
without a self-righteous attitude or complaint.
Thank You for all You have given me.

BENIDA MADILL

There never was any heart truly great and generous
that was not also tender and compassionate.
—Robert Frost[50]

Be completely humble and gentle;
be patient, bearing with one another in love.
Ephesians 4:2

The phone rings and is answered.
"Hello?"
"Winnie?"
With an inner groan, the voice is recognized. "No, Benida. Mom's at the store."
"Winnie?"
"She's at the store."
"Where's Winnie?"
A bit louder this time. "She's at the store!"
"She's doing laundry?"
More emphasis this time. "She's at the STORE!"
"Winnie?"

Full yell now. "MY MOM'S AT THE STORE!"

And so it would continue until the hard-of-hearing caller finally left a message for our mother and hung up.

Benida Madill. Named for her parents, Ben and Ida, this woman had become a permanent fixture in our lives. It started when our parents began a Bible study in our home. A woman named Harriet came for a couple weeks, then began bringing her neighbor, Benida. For some reason Benida latched onto our mother, and a few weeks later, when Harriet stopped coming to Bible study, Benida began calling our mother to come and pick her up.

At first it was just a ride to church or the hairdresser. As years went by, the rides became more frequent. Our mother began doing Benida's mending, then her laundry. Time passed and Mom bathed Benida, took her to doctor's appointments, and attended to her banking. Finally Benida's health was so poor she was admitted to a nursing home. But she fought the staff there and insisted Mom come to bathe her, comb her hair, and see to all her other needs.

You can easily see what a time-consuming job this became for our mother. And perhaps it wouldn't have been so bad if Benida was a grandmotherly and sweet old lady. But she wasn't. An infection in her adult years had robbed Benida of all but the tiniest bit of hearing, and she responded with anger at the world. Although we knew it was true from mementos she showed us, it was hard for us to imagine Benida playing on a girls' basketball team, working as a librarian, earning a graduate degree. To us, she was a crabby old woman who expected our mother to wait on her hand and foot, but griped and complained at every action my mother took.

Despite all the bitterness, demanding phone calls, and tongue-lashings Benida dealt, our mother loved Benida. She welcomed her into our home, insisting she come regularly for meals and for every holiday. Mom gave us a "mind-your-manners" look if we dared to complain about the Jell-O with colored marshmallows that Benida made for every potluck. She played cards with Benida, went to movies with her, steadied her as her steps became unbalanced, and cried with her when life was too hard.

Several years ago Benida passed away. When her will was read, we children were outraged to learn Benida had left everything to the Humane Society and a distant niece whom she'd seen twice in about twenty years. Not even a dime was left to our mother.

Was Mom angry? No. She'd known Benida's plans all along. She took care of Benida out of love, with no expectations. It was never easy, yet Mom's selfless actions demonstrated incredible virtue to us, her children.

We pray we will be as gracious and selfless when we meet the next Benida Madill.

Lord, You made the ultimate sacrifice
for me by sending Your Son.
Help me remember Your example of selfless grace
as I make sacrifices in serving others.

LIFE'S A CIRCUS

It is very good for strength,
to know that someone needs you to be strong.
—Elizabeth Barrett Browning[51]

Humble yourselves, therefore,
under God's mighty hand,
that he may lift you up in due time.
1 Peter 5:6

In our families we have a tradition of going to the circus. Every October, Ringling Brothers and Barnum & Bailey Circus travels through Colorado and we're quick to snatch up our tickets. We hold our breath and peek through our fingers as the tightrope walkers balance on bicycles, chairs, and each other's shoulders. (Why don't they use a net?) We eat way too much cotton candy, washing it down with syrupy sodas. We laugh at the antics of the clowns, especially when they pull spectators from the crowds to participate in the pranks. We ooh and aah over the sparkly costumes, the daredevil stunts, the beauty of the tigers, and the antics of the trained dogs. With three rings of action, it's hard to even know where to look at times. We don't want to miss a thing!

The performers get plenty of applause and have their pictures posted on every imaginable surface. You can buy their stories in the circus program. You can wear their faces on a T-shirt. You can play with dolls and action figures made in their likenesses. It's truly life in the spotlight.

Yet there's another crowd of performers who labor outside the circus spotlight. Dressed in dark coveralls and lurking just at the edge of the action are troupes of workers who are vitally important to the success of those in the spotlight, but who receive no glory, no applause, no recognition. These bands of men are the ones who quickly assemble the fenced ring in which the tigers perform. Then, while our attention is distracted by the trapeze artists, this fence disappears and is replaced by the props needed for the next act. These are the people who linger on the outside of the circus rings, armed with huge shovels to immediately remove any droppings from prancing horses or lumbering elephants. It is these workers who pull the ropes for the glitter-covered girls swinging in the rafters, who tighten the cables that hold the nets under the trapeze, who sweep away the confetti left by crazy clowns.

Without these hardworking laborers, the show could not go on. They are truly as important to the success of the show as the performers in the spotlight. Yet none of them will become famous for this work.

What a wonderful example of humility. Here are people who know the performers would fail without them, yet they don't run out into the lights and take bows alongside the ringmaster or the clowns. They don't demand, "Look at me! I deserve some praise, too!" Instead, they remain out of sight and let others claim the fame.

This reminds us of the church, where there are many parts that must work together in order for the church to function properly. Everyone shakes the pastor's hand as they leave the sanctuary. The choir director gets a pat on the back for her hard work. A soloist is applauded. But what about the nursery worker who rocked a crying baby for two hours, changing diapers and wiping noses with love. What about those who vacuum the halls, clean up the kitchen after "fellowship hour," and mow the church lawn? What kind of recognition do they get? Yet without these willing workers, no one will hear the pastor speak or the choir sing.

The circus workers also remind us of mothers. Women who do the laundry late at night so their sons will be able to wear their favorite football jerseys to school the next day. Women who hound their children to practice the piano so that same child can be applauded at the next recital. Women who get flowers on Mother's Day, but remain out of the spotlight the rest of the year. Women like you.

We applaud mothers everywhere for the humble acts they do out of the view of others. Without you, the world just wouldn't function.

Lord, let me remember who truly is
the creator of all glory—You!

POTATO POWER

I'll huff and I'll puff and I'll blow your house down!
—The Wolf[52]

God chose the weak things
of the world to shame the strong.
1 Corinthians 1:27

Next time you're making mashed potatoes (the real kind . . . like Amy makes, not the instant ones that Jody serves) try this little experiment. Take a plain drinking straw and a raw potato and try to stick the straw through the entire potato. (Go ahead, take a "stab" at it!) You'll likely end up with a crumpled straw, and a new respect for how hard potatoes are! Now, hold your thumb over the end of a new, uncrumpled drinking straw so your thumb covers the hole. Try the experiment again. Voila! You've impaled the potato on the straw with merely the flick of a wrist! (Note: This is a really time-consuming way to make French fries.)

The secret to this "trick" is simply air pressure. When you place your thumb over the straw, you trap air inside the straw. And when that air is forced against the potato, the potato has to give. We generally don't think of plain old air as powerful—until we consider tornadoes or hurricanes. That air that you're inhaling right now is powerful stuff.

Humility is like air. It appears weak, until we see it used in a powerful way. While you're waiting for those potatoes to cook, flip your Bible open to 1 Samuel 25 and read about Abigail. "An intelligent and beautiful woman" (just like all of us, of course!), Abigail had a "surly and mean" husband, Nabal, who's name meant "fool." When Nabal offended David, a man of increasing power and influence, David and his men strapped on their swords and headed for Nabal's home. Who could stop this powerful, angry army from destroying all that Nabal owned? It was Abigail, bearing gifts and humility, who saved Nabal's home. She "bowed low before David, with her face to the ground." Abigail begged for David's forgiveness, praised his God, and wished David success in his endeavors against Saul. Her humility was powerful. So powerful that David's jaw dropped and the swords came down. Humility had stopped an army.

Do you avoid humbling yourself, thinking you might appear weak? What might happen if, instead of boasting, you bowed? How can humility be powerful in your life? How can you demonstrate mighty humility today?

Mighty Lord, I humbly bow before You today.
Use my humble attitude and actions
to do mighty things today.
Give me a meek heart that is willing to serve others.

HUMBLE HEARTS,
HARDWORKING HANDS

Never let a problem to be solved become
more important than a person to be loved.
—Barbara Johnson[53]

I tell you the truth,
anyone who gives you a cup of water
in my name because you belong to Christ
will certainly not lose his reward.
Mark 9:41

Years ago Amy worked with a number of corporate trainers. One morning she was helping one of her coworkers, Dan, prepare for an upcoming meeting.

"I've ordered doughnuts," Dan said. "Will you make the coffee?"

Amy looked at Dan blankly, stammering and stuttering, but not giving any answer. Immediately Dan backpedaled. "I know making coffee isn't in your job description. Never mind, I'll do it. Sorry I asked."

At this, Amy began to laugh. "It's not that I'm not willing to make coffee. It's just that I don't drink coffee, and I'm embarrassed to admit I don't even know how to make it! If you'll show me how, I'll be glad to make it before the meeting."

The situation was resolved, but it shows how petty people have become in our society. We think we'll offend someone just by asking them to make coffee—and it's likely that many people actually *are* offended by simple requests such as these. What ever happened to humility?

When we first began attending our church, we soon met two beautiful women. They were outgoing with great personalities, attractive, and had gorgeous homes. Their hair always looked perfect, their clothes were from upscale shops, and they always had their nails neatly manicured. It seemed to us that these women enjoyed some of the finer things in life.

As we got to know these women, we learned they were partners in a small business. Were they interior designers? Did they own a trendy shop downtown? Had they invested in a local restaurant? No! These women worked together cleaning homes. They were maids! In order to pay for the luxury of having their nails done, as well as to pay for their children's school clothes, make car payments, and contribute to other household expenses, these lovely ladies were daily scrubbing floors and toilets. Most of us can't stand to do these menial chores in our own homes, much less do them for someone else. Yet these women were beautiful not only in appearance—they were beautiful in spirit and in humility as well. They laughed and sang while they worked together, even sharing about Christ to the wealthy women whose homes they were cleaning.

Our mother is a nurse and works in a home for the elderly. Many times she has washed the faces of those who cannot feed themselves and who dribble food and spittle upon themselves. She has cleaned up after those who can no longer control their bowel functions. Instead of saying, "I have a college degree! I'm not getting my hands dirty! Let an orderly do it!" she approaches her patients with love, even when it means doing things others would consider odious.

So few of us have this kind of humility. We might not be blatantly rude about it, but we're never quick to volunteer for those menial tasks we think are beneath us. Oh, if we could remember the attitude of Jesus as He washed the feet of His disciples. Here was God in the form of a man, kneeling before His friends to gently wash their grimy, sweaty, and stinking feet. And when He finished, listen to what He said: "Now that I, your Lord and Teacher, have washed your feet, you also should wash one another's feet. I have set you an example that you should do as I have done for you" (John 13:14–15).

When we hear sermons on this passage, we think, "I want to be a servant." But as soon as someone treats us like one, we're offended. Jesus was the most humble servant. He asks us to serve others with this same kind of love and humility. Let's embrace this virtue with our hearts and our hands.

Lord, You have served me with
more humility than I could ever muster.
Thank You for humbling Yourself,
becoming a man,
and giving Your life for mine.

2 GOOD
2 BE
4GOTTEN

*A girl's best friend
is her mother.*
—Mary Englebreit[54]

*I thank my God
every time I remember you.
In all my prayers for all of you,
I always pray with joy.*
Philippians 1:3–4

Do you remember the day that high school yearbooks came out at your school? What was the first thing you did? Most likely, you quickly flipped the pages to find your picture, and you winced at how badly your hair had turned out that day. Then you scanned the pages to find your friends' pictures (secretly hoping that they looked as dorky as you

117

did) and pictures of that guy you always had a crush on (you know, the one you sat behind in geometry). Yet, one of the best parts of yearbooks was getting them signed by all your friends—and maybe a teacher or two, if no one was looking. You asked people to give some kind of a written record of their relationship with you.

When you think about it, high school yearbooks are funny things. Filled with weighty titles like "Most Popular," "Best Looking," or "Most Likely to Succeed," yearbooks capture both who we were. . .and who we were to become. But they also give insight to how others viewed us.

Flip through your high school yearbook. Although it may be hard to get past the ghastly photos of your funky hairdo, embroidered bell-bottom jeans, or platform shoes, don't look at the pictures. Simply read. Read what people wrote to you and about you. Read the reminders of inside jokes, nicknames, and crushes. Then ask yourself, "What kind of a friend was I?" Were you compassionate—a shoulder others could cry on? Were you funny—always ready to cheer someone up with a joke or silly story? Were you reliable—a friend that anyone could count on? Maybe you'll like the answer. . . maybe you won't.

Now, close your eyes and picture the past year as a yearbook. There are photos of your family, friends, coworkers, neighbors, and even a few acquaintances. (You can go ahead and create titles like "Most Likely to Exceed Her Credit Limit" or "Least Likely to Ever Mow His Lawn." Just keep them all tucked away in your brain!) Think about this question: What would people write to you and about you *now*? What kind of a friend would they say you were? How do you feel about their comments?

> *Loving Lord, thank You for the friends*
> *that You've placed in my life throughout the years.*
> *Help me to be a kind and*
> *compassionate friend in return.*
> *Give me a clear snapshot of the kind of friend*
> *You want me to be.*

ALL THE TIME

Treat your friends as you do your pictures,
and place them in their best light.
—Jennie Jerome Churchill[55]

A friend loves at all times.
Proverbs 17:17

One Sunday after church, Jody and her husband were talking with their almost two-year-old daughter, Brianna.

"What did you do in the nursery?" Jody asked.

"Crying," was Brianna's response. Jody and Erik remembered that when they'd left her, Brianna *was* crying (big crocodile tears, mind you).

"What did you do when you stopped crying?" asked Erik.

Brianna scowled and pushed her hand away from her body. "No, Emily!" she shouted. Jody and Erik gathered that — somehow or another—Brianna and Emily hadn't been getting along.

Brianna has a lot to learn about friendships. Perhaps we all do.

It's so easy to push friends away, carry grudges against them, take them for granted, or lose touch with them. We place conditions on our friendships. "I'll be your friend *if. . .*" How different would our friendships be if, instead, we lived Proverbs 17:17: "A friend loves *at all times*"? Let's see what that might be like:

A friend loves when the other friend's children write all over the couch with red markers.

A friend loves when the other friend consistently makes them late for the movie.

A friend loves when the other friend loses more weight on the diet you started together.

A friend loves when miles and time have kept you from the other friend.

A friend loves when the other friend appears to be growing a mold garden in her shower.

A friend loves when the other friend gives you the same Christmas present you gave her last year.

A friend loves *at all times.*

Gracious Lord, help me to be
a loving and forgiving friend.
Give me Your grace to accept my friends
and to see them through Your eyes.

HELPING HANDS

And when you're outside, looking in,
who's there to open the door?
That's what friends are for!
—the Vultures from *The Jungle Book* [56]

If one falls down, his friend can help him up.
But pity the man who falls
and has no one to help him up!
Ecclesiastes 4:10

A few years ago, Amy's husband, Mike, required unex-pected surgery. Unfortunately, the surgery solved one health problem but created another. While doctors were sorting this out, Mike was sick in bed. For over three months he was unable to work. The inflow of money dwindled while the flow of household and medical bills increased.

On top of it all, Amy and Mike's house was in serious need of painting. After getting several professional estimates (and laughing at the ludicrous idea that they'd be able to pay the painters), Amy began scraping the old paint off herself.

Four days later, barely half of one side of the house was scraped. Says Amy, "It's not that our house is so big. It's just that it was a big job for one person—namely me!"

Then on the fifth day, just after dinner, cars began to drive up to the house. Friends from church piled out of the car wearing old clothes and with scrapers in hand. Ladders were unloaded, cans of primer were opened, and within two hours the entire house was scraped and primer had been painted over all the exposed areas. Wow!

But that's not all! A few days later it was Saturday. A beautiful day when people could be boating at the lake, playing at a park, hiking in the mountains. Instead, cars showed up again, and the painting began. Not only were these friends so generous that they twice gave of their time for this chore, they even brought the paint, paintbrushes, and other supplies, plus gave Mike and Amy a gift of money they'd collected!

At the end of the day brushes were washed out, tired muscles stretched, and everyone stood back to admire the house coated in new shades of blue.

What an incredible and tangible expression of love in the family of God! When one member was weak, others were strong. And what a humbling experience for Mike. At least Amy could be out working alongside these giving friends. Mike, on the other hand, had to stay inside, resting in bed and reading a book, knowing his friends were slaving outside on his behalf.

The neighbors were amazed, too. Who was this group of people who cheerfully laughed and joked while swinging paintbrushes all day? Why were they doing this? These questions opened the doors for Amy and Mike to tell their neighbors what wonderful friends God had given them through the family of God.

Eventually Mike's health improved enough for him to begin working again. He and Amy told everyone who would listen about their incredible friends, knowing they could never repay this act of service and love.

The story could end there, but there's one last bit to be told. Nearly a year later, Amy was looking through the papers their son, Tony, had brought home from Bible class. There was a handout called "Helping Hands." On this Tony had drawn a picture of himself painting a house the exact shades of blue his home now was. Beside it the instructions read, "Write a way you might help others when you grow up." Tony had written, "Help paint somebody's house."

The legacy these friends left continues.

Heavenly Father, thank You for friends
who express love in ways
I never can repay.

STICKY SISTERS

*Friendship is the only cement
that will ever hold the world together.*
—Woodrow Wilson [57]

*Whoever welcomes one of these
little children in my name welcomes me.*
Mark 9:37

Our sister, Jill, is always sending silly stories, jokes, and interesting tidbits via e-mail. Recently she forwarded a list of actual headlines from today's newspapers. Maybe they'll make you giggle as much as we did:

Include Your Children When Baking Cookies
Police Begin Campaign to Run Down Jaywalkers
Drunk Gets Nine Months in Violin Case
Eye Drops Off Shelf
Enraged Cow Injures Farmer With Ax
Miners Refuse to Work After Death

Two Sisters Reunited After 18 Years in Checkout Counter

Jill knows that we are "word people" who enjoy a good misplaced modifier (and who doesn't?). Since Jill understands our sense of humor, her e-mail messages not only make us grin, but they help us grow together as sisters and as friends.

Simple thoughtful gestures, like an e-mail message, a phone call, or a cup of coffee go a long way toward making friendships stronger. In fact, they're almost essential to maintaining a deep and meaningful friendship. We often hear "it's the little things that count," but do we live that phrase in our relationships?

After graduating from college, Jody moved to southern California to teach at a Christian school. She didn't have much money and things were tight. Plus, she really missed her family. "I'll never forget the day I got that package from Amy, Mike, and Tony," she writes. "It was a huge box filled with lots of little things—soap, cookies, toothpaste, and cotton balls. I remember holding the box of Fig Newtons and sobbing because they even remembered to get the fat-free kind!" That little gesture will never be forgotten.

Thoughtfulness isn't reserved for our adult friendships. Kids enjoy little things, too. Include a favorite treat in your child's lunch box—just because it's his favorite. Is your daughter a big Barbie fan? An inexpensive package of Barbie stickers will mean a lot. After your child has had a rough day, give him a break from his chores to say, "I understand how you feel." Not only will you be building a stronger friendship with your kids, you're showing them how to be a thoughtful and considerate friend. After all, those "little things" will soon be "big things."

Holy Father, I want to know my children
better and show them that I understand.
Open my eyes to the little things
I can do that will build a strong friendship.

I NEVER KNEW!

Always sisters, always friends.
Let's stay real close 'til the end.
—CeCe, Debbie, and Angie Winans[58]

I no longer call you servants,
because a servant does not know
his master's business. Instead,
I have called you friends,
for everything that I learned from my Father
I have made known to you.
John 15:15

How well do you know your friends? Or how well do your friends know you? You've spent countless hours with your friends, eating chocolate, sipping diet sodas, shopping, complaining about day care, laughing over funny things your kids have said, and on and on. But do you really know each other? Have you gone beyond talking about the latest fashions, politics, or child care theories and opened your heart?

Sometimes we can spend years as friends and not know

basic facts about our friends such as their favorite colors or holidays. For example, after seven years of close camaraderie, Amy discovered one of her friends colors her hair. Even though they'd spent incredible amounts of time together, Amy never knew this little detail. (I'm sure some of you are wondering what magician colors this woman's hair so perfectly!)

Or on a deeper level, do you know how your friends first learned about God? What they pray about? How they're growing spiritually? There's so much more to learn!

Recently our sister Jill sent us a friendship questionnaire. She'd already filled it out, telling us both trivial and important information about her. Jill was letting us in on more of her life. She asked that we would fill out the questionnaire with answers about ourselves and send this back to her. She wanted to be in on more of our lives as well.

What a wonderful and risky idea! You've opened yourself up first, not knowing what your friends will think about you after learning these facts. Then you ask them to open their lives to you as well. Yet how can a friendship grow deeper unless we're willing to expose our hearts?

We've compiled a Friendship Questionnaire of our own for you to use. Some questions are on the lighter side, and some will make you think. Share the answers to these questions with your friends, and ask them to share their answers with you.

Nicknames?
Favorite salad dressing?
Do you color your hair?
Favorite colors?

Besides God, who are you looking forward to
    seeing in heaven?
Favorite season?
Favorite type of music?
How did you become a Christian?
Dream vacation?
Favorite food?
Are you a hopeless romantic or a nonromantic?
Do you get along with your parents?
Favorite town to visit?
What's one dream for your future?
Did you play in any high school sports?
Favorite subject in school?
Least favorite subject?
What's one thing you fear?
Favorite sport?
Favorite holiday?
What do you look for in a friend?

Now, how well can you answer these questions as they
relate to your family? You know your son hates squash, but do
you know his dreams? You could name your daughter's favorite
athletes in your sleep, but do you know what kind of friend she
longs to have? Go deeper. You'll never regret it.

All-knowing God,
You have opened Your heart
and welcomed me as a daughter and friend.
Give me the encouragement I need to do likewise.

BOUQUET OF FRIENDSHIP

Flowers have spoken to me more
than I can tell in written words.
They are the hieroglyphics of angels,
loved by all men for the beauty of the character,
though few can decipher
even fragments of their meaning.
—Lydia M. Child[59]

Flowers appear on the earth;
the season of singing has come,
the cooing of doves is heard in our land.
Song of Songs 2:12

If you're like us, you love to receive a bouquet of flowers. Whether it's roses from the nervous hand of a beau or a bunch of dandelions clutched in the muddy fingers of a child, almost every woman loves to get flowers.

Did you know flowers, herbs, fruits, and other plants have symbolic meanings? Most people simply choose flowers for their beauty, color, or scent. However, long ago a variety of meanings were attached to various plants. Receiving these bits of vegetation could send a message. A rose would represent love, while basil would stand for hate. A bouquet would take on a whole new meaning!

It won't surprise anyone to learn apples represent temptation. So next time you take a bowl of fruit as a hostess gift, consider the meaning of that apple before you place it on top. You would certainly want to include a pear, as it stands for affection, and a peach will really boost your friend's ego as it means, "Your qualities, like your charms, are unequaled." Think again before you add a pomegranate, as it signifies foolishness, or raspberries, which represent remorse.

As the apple is aptly symbolized, so is the Venus flytrap, which embodies its meaning of deceit. And the lily of the valley, which so many associate with Easter, is appropriate in meaning "return of happiness." But how did cool peppermint come to mean "warmth of feeling"? And stranger still, what crazed mind determined a cactus would symbolize warmth?

Think of your friends. Think of the qualities and virtues that endear them to you. Then consider these plants as you gather flowers to create a bouquet to represent your friendship:

- Red chrysanthemums symbolize love
- White chrysanthemums stand for truth
- White daisies represent innocence
- Ferns connote sincerity
- Hyacinths stand for game, sport, or play
- An iris means "message"
- Marigolds represent grief

- Nasturtiums stand for patriotism
- Zinnia means "thoughts of absent friends"
- Holly connotes foresight

So head to the fields or the florist. Select the flowers and plants that best represent the virtues of your friends. Tie your bouquets together with ivy, as with its weaving and winding ways it represents the bonds of friendship. Present these to your friends with an explanation of what the flowers and your relationship means.

Then choose one or two flowers for your children, and do the same for them. It's never too early to begin cultivating the roots of friendship. And don't forget to toss in a sprig of mint. It stands for virtue.[60]

Lord, You have created each flower,
each fragrance, and each friendship.
Let me blossom in friendship
as others see Your love in me.

LEFTOVERS

A Christian will find it cheaper
to pardon than to resent.
Forgiveness saves the expense of anger,
the cost of hatred, the waste of spirits.
—Hannah Moore[61]

Bear with each other and
forgive whatever grievances
you may have against one another.
Forgive as the Lord forgave you.
Colossians 3:13

Everything leaves a trace. Goldilocks left half-eaten porridge, a broken chair, and rumpled bedspreads. Toddlers leave sticky handprints on everything they touch. Some people leave a delightful reminder of their Chanel No. 5 in a room. Husbands often leave whiskers and shaving cream in the sink. Rain leaves puddles and mud, but it also leaves rainbows.

When our family lived in southern California, rain often left something else. "As a little girl, I remember watching snails

134

ooze across the sidewalk after a rainstorm," says Jody. "Now, snails aren't the most interesting creatures to watch, but I loved the shiny 'stuff' (for lack of a more knowledgeable term) that they left behind. It was iridescent, shiny, and no other animal that I knew of could do that. It wasn't the snails that caught my eye—they were actually kind of gross! But what they left behind was beautiful to a four-year-old."

Like rainstorms, snails, and Goldilocks, we will all leave something behind—a sign to others that we've touched their lives. What will you leave behind? What "stuff" will show the path you've taken? Will it be a trail of harsh words woven through a child's mind? Or will it be memories of loving actions etched on the heart of loved ones? Will it be rich, meaningful traditions that honor God? Or will you leave behind marks of indifference and unforgiveness. You have a choice.

On December 1, 1997, fourteen-year-old Michael Carneal chose to leave a mark of death, loss, and hate when he opened fire on a group of Christian students at Heath High School. It's extremely likely that that is what Michael will be remembered for. The lives he touched are forever scarred.

Missy Jenkins chose differently. Missy, who was hit by one of Michael's bullets and is now paralyzed, has chosen to forgive. Her forgiveness, a conscious decision, has left a powerful impression on the world that watched the tragedy from afar. She says, "My family and I have been surprised at the attention the media has focused on us. They especially want to know how we could forgive him. But as Christians, it's what God expects us to do. . . . I also feel this happened for a reason. A lot of people have told me my good attitude has been an inspiration to them."[62]

Like all of us, Missy and Michael made choices about what they will leave behind. They've left their mark on the world in two very different ways. Where Michael left a deep, painful scar, Missy has left a shining trail of a godly heart. And her forgiveness will touch the world.

Dear Lord, give me a forgiving heart.
I want to leave a mark of godliness and forgiveness.
I know that may be hard sometimes,
so help me to make the conscious choice.

A DAY AT THE OFFICE

Once a woman has forgiven her man,
she must not reheat his sins for breakfast.
—Marlene Dietrich[63]

This is how my heavenly Father will treat each of you
unless you forgive your brother from your heart.
Matthew 18:35

The boss wants to see you!"

This was the first thing Joani heard when she showed up for work one Monday morning. And it was the last thing she wanted to hear.

"You called for me?" Joani hesitantly questioned as she stood before her employer, Mr. Beckman.

"Yes, Joani. I've been talking with accounting, and they pointed out a major problem. You've been managing funds for my company for the past three years and in that time have lost nearly ten million dollars!"

Hanging her head in misery, Joani replied, "I know. . . . It was foolish spending, bad investments, and more. I don't know what to tell you."

"I know what you should tell me. Tell me you're going to have to repay this money!" Mr. Beckman demanded.

"You know I can't!"

"Then I'll have to confiscate everything you own. Your house will be sold, along with all your possessions. And that's only going to cover a tiny portion of this debt. You're going to have to permanently become a servant in my home to pay back what you owe. In fact, your entire family will have to work for me!"

It was more than she could bear. Joani fell to the floor crying.

"No! I beg of you, please don't punish me like this! It's more than I can take!"

Mr. Beckman thought for a few minutes, then surprised everyone by suddenly changing his mind.

"Fine. You can go. I won't make you repay this. We'll manage the loss somehow. Now you'd better get back to work."

Stunned but thrilled, Joani quickly straightened her dress, smoothed her hair, and headed to her desk.

Just as she was turning on her computer, Bonnie walked past.

"Hi Joani!" she cheerfully began.

"Bonnie! You thief!" Joani spouted out in anger.

Dazed, Bonnie just stood there.

"I loaned you money for donuts last Friday and you haven't paid me back yet. I'm calling the police this very minute to have you arrested and put in jail until you pay me back!"

Ungrateful Joani. Pardoned of her crimes that totaled in

the millions, she cannot forget the debt of a few quarters owed to her. "This would never happen," you say. Sure it would. It happens all the time.

We've retold a parable of Jesus from Matthew 18. A king wipes away the debt of a servant who owes him an incredible amount, yet this servant cannot forget another who owes him a tiny bit of money. In turn, the king decides not to forgive the first servant after all. The meaning is clear. God has forgiven us of our incredible debt of sin. Yet we find it difficult to forgive others of their sins against us.

Ungrateful us. Pardoned of our sins that total in the millions, we cannot forget the few sins against us. Like we said, it happens all the time.

Who do you need to forgive? Is it someone at work? At home? An estranged relative?

We say of our God, "He is a merciful and forgiving God. He is our example." Let your children say of their mother, "She's merciful and forgiving." And by your example, they will be, too.

Father, help me to forgive
as You have forgiven me.

JOIN THE CLUB

Christians aren't perfect—Just forgiven.
—seen on a bumper sticker

For all have sinned and fall short
of the glory of God,
and are justified freely by his grace.
Romans 3:23–24

Parents magazine often runs a humorous column titled "I Can't Believe I Did That!" The feature is basically a forum for parents to admit to their "less-than-perfect parenthood moments."[64] These confessions often come from desperate, sleep-deprived parents who do things such as start on a trip with all the baby accessories—stroller, diaper bag, baby seat, portable crib—but accidentally leave the baby at home. One fatigued mother shared how she wearily stumbled into her toddler's room to comfort him late at night. For some reason, her efforts to soothe the child were ineffective. . . until she realized she was holding him upside down! Another mother wrote about buying a new pair of shoes for her young son. When the boy protested that his feet hurt, she busily told him to stop whining, assuming that the shoes needed to be broken in. Several hours later, when the toddler wouldn't stop complaining about his feet, the mother took the shoes off and realized that they still had the paper in the toes. The boy had been tightly curling up his toes for hours! Each month, parents share their blunders and shortcomings, initiating themselves into the "Imperfect Parents Club," of which most—if not all—of us are members. Life-long members.

Sharing our goofs and gaffes with other members of the Imperfect Parents Club may be embarrassing, but at least there we're safe from judgment or harsh criticism. Most members will respond by shaking their heads and saying, "If you think *that's* bad, wait 'til you hear what *I* did!" It's a very forgiving bunch. Until it comes to nonmembers. . .primarily children.

Face it, kids sure make a lot of mistakes (just like we do). They spill Kool-Aid on our income tax papers. They accidentally discover that you can't flush an entire roll of toilet paper down the toilet at one time. They slip and say bad words in front of our church leaders. They mistake the feelings of fatigue for feelings of defiance and anger, resulting in tantrums. They err by smearing Vaseline on Grandma's flocked wallpaper (how were they supposed to know it wouldn't come off?).

Maybe we need to let kids in on the secrets of the Imperfect Parents Club. Tell your kids about the time you fed the baby pizza because you were just too tired to peel and mush up a banana. Confess to the six-month stretch when you let your toddler watch *The Tonight Show* because it put him to sleep. Admit that you were the one who left the red sock in the white laundry, then bleached everything beyond recognition. ("Really, gray is a very popular color these days!") Most importantly, tell about times when someone forgave you for those imperfections. What was that like? How did it make you feel? Did it make it easier for you to forgive others?

Our children so often need our forgiveness. We forget that we also need theirs. Forgiveness can be hard to dish out. But aren't you grateful when someone dishes it your way?

Forgiving Father, help me to forgive
the errors that my children make.
Help me to remember the times others forgave me.
May I show Your grace and forgiveness
as I remember all that You have pardoned in my life.

STAY IN THE GAME

I'll be there for you.
—The Rembrandts[65]

A faithful man will be richly blessed.
Proverbs 28:20

What will it take for Coach Kay Dalton to miss a game? The world may never know. Shortly before the University of Northern Colorado football team was to play an important game, sixty-six-year-old Dalton dislocated his hip.[66] "I've never been shot, but it felt the way you'd expect it to if you were shot," he recalls. In spite of the incredible pain, he adamantly refused to go to the hospital for surgery. "I have a game to call," he said firmly. The team physician was forced to perform emergency surgery in the locker room, then give Dalton a drug to reverse the effects of the anesthesia. Dalton scoffed at those who wanted to carry him upstairs to the press box. So moments after hip surgery, Kay Dalton grabbed a crutch and tackled three flights of stairs on his own so he could call the game. He only missed the first play.

You may think a man like Coach Dalton is simply stubborn. But his players were touched and inspired by his loyalty and commitment. "He is the toughest man I know," one said. "If he can do what he did and come back and call the game, the least we could do was win it for him." And so they did.

Your faithfulness and loyalty will speak volumes to those who depend on you. Loyalty shows that you put a high priority on others—that you are devoted to them in any circumstance. Our grandmother faithfully cared for our grandfather, who was diagnosed with Alzheimer's. Her devotion was a clear picture of her love for him.

Loyalty also sets a high standard for others to follow. Although all of us kids saw our parents struggle at different times in their marriage, we knew that their commitment to each other was strong. That message has carried over into our strong commitment to our spouses. We had a powerful example to follow.

Most of all, loyalty shows the heart of God. Throughout the Bible, God is called "faithful." When you display loyalty—to a spouse, to children, to a task, or even to your country—you are giving others a glimpse of God's faithfulness to His people.

So don't hesitate to get back into the game. There are a lot of players out there waiting for you to guide them to victory!

Faithful Lord, help me to set aside my own needs
to be loyal to those who depend on me.
Let me show them a bit of Your heart
through my faithfulness.

HOUND DOG FAITHFULNESS

I want my boy to have a dog
To be his pal and friend,
So he may learn that friendship
Is faithful to the end.
—Marty Hale[67]

Because of the Lord's great love
we are not consumed,
for his compassions never fail.
They are new every morning;
great is your faithfulness.
Lamentations 3:22–23

A favorite book in both of our homes is the children's book *Good Dog, Carl* by Alexandra Day. In this picture book (and its many sequels), a mother leaves her baby with the family dog, a Rottweiler named Carl, while she runs errands. The adventure begins the second the door closes and baby Madeleine climbs on Carl's back. The two roam the house—playing dress up, jumping on the bed, dancing, making snacks, taking a bath, and sliding down the laundry chute. Through it all, Carl cleans up the mess, makes the bed, carries Madeleine, and helps her back into bed just before the mother opens the door. And for all his efforts, he receives a pat on the head and the three little words, "Good dog, Carl."[68]

One of the traits that makes the *Carl* books so endearing is Carl's complete devotion and loyalty to Madeleine. Carl knows that it's his job to care for Madeleine. Doggie treats aren't lavished on him. He doesn't get his belly scratched. And I doubt he's in it for the generous praises poured upon him. His loyalty is part of his nature—part of his love for his master.

Amy's son has a dog, Aladdin, who has something in common with Carl. They're both black. That's where it ends. Aladdin isn't a loyal, faithful dog. In fact, Aladdin tries to run away any chance he's given. Aladdin probably enjoys his chew toys, playing with Tony, and sleeping in a warm bed inside a warm house, but you wouldn't say that he is loyal to his master. (Although he's great at cuddling and Amy rarely has to mop since he's always there to "clean up" after her!)

We've all had "Aladdins" in our lives—people who are there for the fun times but look for an opportunity to scram when the going gets rough. But we all have had "Carls" in our lives, too. Who has been a faithful, loyal influence in your life? Was it a teacher, who went the extra mile when you were hopelessly behind? Or did you have a Sunday school teacher who faithfully prayed for you during your childhood and adolescence? Maybe you had a best friend who never turned her back on you—even when you deserved it.

How do you show loyalty to those in your life? Do you

believe in your children? Do friends know, without a doubt, that they can call on you in times of trouble? Does your family believe that they are first in your life?

Like Carl, you have opportunities every day to show loyalty to those around you. It may be hard work. Some people might not even realize you've done anything! But unlike Carl, your Master sees what you're doing. And He is saying, "Well done, good and faithful servant!"

Holy God, help me to be
a faithful servant today.
May my actions be
done well in Your sight.

HANDLE WITH CARE

It's been said that God gave us
things to use and people to enjoy.
People without friends use people and enjoy things.
—Dale Evans Rogers[69]

The Lord is faithful to all his promises
and loving toward all he has made.
Psalm 145:13

Mom! Dad broke the coffee table!"
This call came up from Amy's basement playroom recently. She remembers, "I was upstairs enjoying a few quiet minutes of reading while my husband and son were downstairs watching an Elvis Presley movie—they're both big Elvis fans. I could barely hear them singing along and laughing together. Suddenly they both came thundering up the stairs, with Tony yelling about his dad breaking the coffee table. It turns out that Mike was in the middle of doing one of his Elvis impersonations and jumped up onto the coffee table to use it as a stage. No sooner had he begun his rendition of 'Jailhouse Rock,' than

the table split in two, right down the middle. Well, the damage was already done, so I shrugged, told them to clean up the mess and be more careful, and went back to my reading."

Does this seem like too casual of a response to you? Perhaps it was, but Amy learned long ago that possessions come and go and she should hold them loosely. It's people that really matter. After all, most objects can be repaired or replaced. Relationships. . .well, that's another matter.

So many of us show incredible loyalty to our possessions, yet fail to give that same care and consideration to our friends, and even less to our family members. Think about some of your "nice" things. Do you polish your few pieces of silver with the softest cloth available? Do you keep your china hidden away to be used only on the most special occasion, and even then treat these delicate dishes with the utmost care? Do you have rules such as "No shoes on the couch," or "No jumping on the beds"? It's likely these are all true. And to be honest, we're not saying you should trash your belongings. We should take care of what God's given to us. But shouldn't we extend that same care to our friends and especially to our families? After all, God gave us these, too.

Both of us have had friendships that were strong for years, but then a few angry words were spoken or a misunderstanding was never cleared up, and the friendships were never the same. We considered ourselves loyal and true friends, yet failed to properly mend what had been torn.

And how many times has each of us spoken harshly to our husbands, yelled at our kids, or simply failed to treat our family members with kindness and respect. We say our families are important to us, but often our words and actions fall short of showing this to be true. We give more honor to our antique dishes than to our children.

Amy's son Tony was visiting our parents a few years ago and was fascinated by some very old tools and books that had belonged to our grandfather before he passed away. While handling these items, he accidentally broke something. He fearfully approached our father, worried at what his punishment would be. After all, this item could never be replaced.

"Grandpa, I broke this. . .I'm sorry. . . ," Tony began, holding out the pieces.

Our father took Tony in his arms and forgave him. Instead of the spanking he deserved, Dad remembered that the heart of a child is more fragile than an antique tool. His loyalty was to his grandson, not to his possessions.

Can we say the same?

Heavenly Father, You never fail me,
even when I am a failure.
Help me to be gracious and remain loyal
when others fall short of my expectations.

GO TEAM!

I'll love you forever,
I'll like you for always.
As long as I'm living,
my baby you'll be.
—Robert Munsch[70]

Be devoted to one another. . . .
Honor one another above yourselves.
Romans 12:10

Jody's husband, Erik, is a fervent UCLA sports fan. And that's putting it mildly. He has countless UCLA paraphernalia—sweatshirts, T-shirts, hats, mugs. . .even a UCLA pillow! He visits the UCLA football Web page almost daily. He reads up on the football and basketball teams—learning the names of their players and all their stats (yet he can't remember where we keep the toilet paper. . .hmmmm?). Erik wouldn't dream of missing a game and calls the cable company to complain when they aren't showing one. And watching each game is an aerobic workout—jumping, yelling, falling down, clapping, and cheering. No one

151

would doubt that Erik is devoted to his team.

What would it be like if we all were so loyal and devoted to our kids? Maybe you wake up in the morning and make the bed (sheets embroidered with your children's initials), stumble out of your pajamas, and put on your kids' favorite colors. Instead of the newspaper, you reach for your child's homework to read over. (Wow, he wrote an entire essay on pizza. Must be his favorite.) Later in the day, you're practically jumping up and down with excitement, knowing that you get to see your kids after school! And when they tell you the play-by-play of the kid who threw up in homeroom, you listen with rapt attention.

Okay, so maybe that's taking it a little far, but you get the idea. What would it be like? An interesting thing about Erik's team loyalty. . .he got it from his dad. Erik's dad and brothers were all big UCLA fans as far back as he can remember. What effect would your "home team" loyalty have on your kids? There's a good chance they'd carry on the tradition.

So be a loyal and devoted fan of your children. Show them that you're wild about them. Be sure they know that you're cheering for them. And never be a "fair-weather fan"; you know, the ones who only support the team when the team is winning. You may shake your head and ask yourself, "When will they ever get this play right?" But don't give up. When they *do* get it right, you'll be standing on the sidelines chanting, "We're number one!"

Faithful Father, thank You for
the "home team" You've given me.
May I be a loyal and
supportive fan in all seasons.

PROMISES, PROMISES

"Goodbye," said the fox.
"And now here is my secret, a very simple secret:
It is only with the heart that one can see rightly;
what is essential is invisible to the eye."
"What is essential is invisible to the eye,"
the little prince repeated,
so that he would be sure to remember.
—Antoine de Saint-Exupéry [71]

I have sought your face with all my heart;
be gracious to me according to your promise.
Psalm 119:58

Where you go I will go, and where you stay I will stay. Your people will be my people and your God my God. Where you die I will die, and there I will be buried. May the Lord deal with me, be it ever so severely, if anything but death separates you and me" (Ruth 1:16–17).

This passage of Scripture is often printed on wedding invitations or heard as a part of the wedding ceremony. But taken in its biblical context, it has nothing to do with romance. These were the words of commitment spoken by a young woman to her mother-in-law. Her mother-in-law?

Let's go back in history a bit. A woman named Naomi, her husband, and two sons left their home in Bethlehem during a time of famine and went to live in Moab. They were there for a number of years, and during this time the sons married women from Moab. Time passed and Naomi's husband and both her sons died. The famine in Bethlehem passed, and Naomi decided to return to her home. The daughters-in-law followed along. But Naomi knew these young women would be considered strangers in Bethlehem. They didn't have the same religious beliefs and would always be thought of as outsiders. Naomi sent them back to their mothers. One of them obeyed, and one did not. Ruth refused to leave Naomi. Perhaps she had seen something of God in Naomi and wanted to know more. Perhaps she had come to love her mother-in-law. We don't know her reasons, but we do know that Ruth pledged to follow Naomi with this strong promise.

And so these two widowed women made their way to Bethlehem. You'll notice as you read the Book of Ruth that she is continually referred to as Ruth the Moabitess. She was always the outsider. But she was faithful to the promise she made to her mother-in-law. She began to work in the fields, gathering bits of grain left behind by the reapers. Her hard work earned her a reputation, and she gained the attention of the owner of the field, a godly man named Boaz. The rest of the story turns into a sort of romance, as Boaz seeks to protect and provide for Ruth and Naomi and Naomi acts as a matchmaker between Ruth and Boaz. Here's what Naomi asks Ruth to do: "Wash and perfume yourself, and put on your best clothes. Then go down to the threshing floor, but don't let him know you are there until he has finished eating and drinking. When he lies down, note the place where he is lying. Then go and uncover his feet and lie down" (Ruth 3:3–4).

Would you do this? Imagine yourself in Ruth's shoes. You've followed your mother-in-law to a new home where you're thought of as an outsider. You do your best to care for this woman you've come to love, even humbling yourself and gathering food along with the poor. Then she makes this crazy request of you. Follow this rich guy to a party, and when he goes to sleep, lie down by his feet. Would you obey? As strange as it sounded, Ruth was loyal to Naomi and obeyed. The end result was the marriage of Ruth and Boaz, and a son from this union named Obed, who became the grandfather of David. Ruth, the outsider, was the great-grandmother of David, and through him, part of the lineage of Jesus Christ.

You may feel God is making unreal or unusual demands of you. You might even be saying to God, "You want me to do *what*?" In your confusion, look at the example of Ruth. She was loyal to her promises, loyal to her mother-in-law, and loyal in her relationships. Her loyalty didn't make life a piece of cake, but it did bring incredible rewards. You may not see the rewards of your actions immediately, but we'll bet your children will.

Faithful Lord, thank You for always staying beside me.
Put godly women in my life that I may follow,
and let me be a godly woman
that my children may follow as well.

DEBORAH: JUDGE, POET, AND ACTION HERO

Injustice anywhere is
a threat to justice everywhere.
—Martin Luther King, Jr. [72]

But you must return to your God;
maintain love and justice,
and wait for your God always.
Hosea 12:6

Scenes from upcoming movies:
James Bond gets the order to take out an international terrorist. He balks. "I'll only go if Deborah goes with me."

Rambo hears of prisoners stranded behind enemy lines. Instead of rushing to their rescue, he begs permission for Deborah to accompany him.

The Terminator is up against warlords of the future. Before he flexes one pectoral muscle, he pleads, "Send Deborah with me!"

You may wonder, "Who's this incredible Deborah, the latest star of action and adventure movies?"

Okay, we admit, she's no action hero of the present, but if anyone were making a movie of the Old Testament, specifically the Book of Judges, that's exactly how one scene would be played. Just watch. . .

SCENE ONE: An ancient city in the desert. A palm tree sways in a tiny breeze, and we see Deborah (played by, hmmm, you always wanted to be in pictures. You can play Deborah!), sitting under the palm tree with a small crowd around her. She's a judge and leader who speaks the words of God. With heavenly guidance she's more decisive than Judge Judy and quickly settles a variety of disputes.

Enter Barak—played by Harrison Ford. The dialogue begins:

Barak: You sent for me?
Deborah: The Lord, the God of Israel, commands you to
        take ten thousand men and head for Mount Tabor.
        God will lure Sisera, a cruel leader of the dreaded
        Canaanites who are oppressing us, and give him
        into your hands.
Barak: (shuffling his feet and stammering) I'll only go if
        you go, too.
Deborah: Very well. But since you've got this kind of atti-
        tude, God's going to give the victory to a woman
        instead of you.

SCENE TWO: Battle scene between the smaller army of Israel and the huge army of Sisera, complete with 900 chariots. God sends a thunderstorm, and the chariots become bogged down in the mud. The Canaanites begin to flee as the army of God chases them down. (Close your eyes during all this blood and gore.)

Cut to Sisera, leader of the Canaanite army, sneaking away from the battle.

SCENE THREE: Sisera, fleeing the battle, comes to a tent of the nomadic Kenites, who, Sisera remembers, are on friendly terms with Canaan. What he forgets is the Kenites have intermarried with the Israelites. . . . The tent belongs to Jael (played by your best girlfriend).

Jael: Come right in! Don't be afraid.
Sisera: I'm thirsty. Please bring me some water.
Jael: I can do even better than that. Here's some milk.

Sisera drinks the milk, Jael brings him a blanket, and he lies down to rest.

Sisera: Stand in the doorway and if anyone comes by
looking for me, tell them you haven't seen me.

Jael stands by the door and waits until Sisera falls asleep. Then she takes a hammer and a tent peg and drives the peg through Sisera's head, into the ground, killing him. (Close your eyes here, too.)

Just then Barak comes running up, chasing after Sisera. Jael brings him in and shows him the body of their enemy.

Justice has been served.
Fade to black, roll credits.

So that's why all these tough guys would want Deborah on their side. (They probably should start clamoring for Jael to join their forces, too.) But who they truly should join forces with is God, the true Hero who brings justice.

Life still isn't perfect. There are injustices in the world today. Huge injustices such as war and persecution, all the way down to the small injustices of the kid who bullies your child on the playground. Unlike Deborah and Jael, we are not led to war and murder. But God still desires us to act justly. What does this mean for you? Do you stand for justice in your home, your workplace, your community?

God's not looking for action heroes, just willing hearts.

Lord, open my eyes
to injustices around me
and give me strength
to stand for what is right.

KIDS' COURT

Even when we fall, He loves us through it all.
His gentle guiding hand keeps understanding.
He knows the tears we cry,
He knows our hearts may lie,
for us again He'd die.
That's what love is.
—John Elefante[73]

I walk in the way of righteousness,
along the paths of justice.
Proverbs 8:20

Imagine this courtroom scene:
The judge is seated, and the first defendant comes forward.

"What have you done?" the judge demands.

"I ran a stoplight," the man confesses.

With a sigh of exasperation, the judge growls at him, "This is the third time you've been in here this week! If you don't stop running lights, I'm going to have to punish you! Now clean up your act and get out of here!"

She waves him away with an angry gesture, and the next person approaches the bench.

"What have you done?" the judge again demands.

"I stole some stuff," the woman admits.

"I've warned you about this. Off to jail with you until I calm down!" the judge orders. The woman slinks away. Another criminal approaches.

"Well?"

"I ran a stoplight, too."

"Another speedster. I'm sick and tired of you guys. Off with your head!"

This judge sounds more like the Queen of Hearts from *Alice in Wonderland* than any judge we've seen. Her judgments are arbitrary, her punishments inconsistent. However, she does sound a lot like mothers we know.

We hear mothers threaten, "If you keep up that whining, we're leaving the store." Half an hour later, we see this same harried woman, stuffing donuts into her child's mouth as she continues her shopping. Her child knew she wasn't going to leave the store, and so did she. Instead of being just, she gave in.

We hear mothers assert, "No dessert until your plate is clean." And after we've all left the table, we see this woman scooping ice cream for the child who left mounds of vegetables uneaten on his plate. He'd been through this routine before and knew he'd win in the end.

We've heard mothers suddenly swoop down on their children screaming, "That's the last straw! You're grounded for the rest of your life!" The child might have merely spilled her milk, but after a day of other frustrations, this mother is frazzled and impatient. Her judgment is swift and harsh.

We expect judges to be fair. If a law is broken, we have set punishments our society believes fit the crime. Pay a fine. Do community service. Spend time in prison. Sure, there are times when the "system" doesn't work or seems unfair, but for the most part, we are disciplined according to our actions.

Unfortunately, we don't always mete out this same form of justice with our children. Our discipline of them can be determined by how bad or good a day we had at work. Or we may be swayed from justice by guilt, thinking, "What will other shoppers think of me if my kid keeps on crying? I'll give in this time and buy him that toy—anything to keep him quiet!" We may show partiality to our children, punishing the one we *assume* is guilty or showing favoritism in our treatment. What kind of justice is this?

We're human. We make mistakes. And we definitely need to ask our children for forgiveness when we've erred. But we must at least strive to be just as we discipline our children. The Bible has plenty of examples of parents who showed favoritism among their children and the results always included heartbreak. The Bible is clear in stating that children need discipline and training. The Bible tells us that God is a just God— he will punish those who deserve it.

Here's the good part. We all deserve punishment. However, God offers us grace and forgiveness. So even though we deserve death, God offers life. That's truly justice gone awry! But until that day of judgment, we should endeavor to be consistent in our discipline. We should let the punishment fit the crime. Your kids may cry, "That's not fair!" Yet if our efforts are truly for justice, they'll know fairness is in your heart. You'll be showing it with your actions.

Forgiving and Just Father,
thank You for remaining constant
in Your justice and in Your love.
Give me wisdom to justly
discipline my children in love.

WEEDS, WORRIES, AND SISTERS WHO SEEM TO GET OUT OF EVERYTHING

Justice. . .limps along, but it gets there all the same.
—Gabriel García Márquez[74]

Lord, don't you care that my sister
has left me to do the work by myself?
Tell her to help me!
Luke 10:40

Other people have "I-walked-twenty-miles-to-school-uphill-in-the-snow-without-any-shoes-carrying-both-of-my-brothers-on-my-back" stories. The Wakefield kids have weeding stories. In our house, Saturday mornings were known for two things: mom's pancakes and weeding. The pancakes were probably a peace offering (or a bribe) because we all detested weeding. All five of us would file out into the backyard, armed with screwdrivers to help penetrate the rock-hard Arizona granite. Of course we all thought Dad was trying to

164

make us better understand the position of the Israelite slaves. (To this day he still says that's not true.) For what seemed like hours, we sweated while we chipped away at the soil, trying to extricate the oh-so-important root of the weed.

But every Saturday, something strange would happen. After about twelve seconds of weeding, Amy would announce that she was headed inside to do the dishes. Into the cool house. Where her hands would get to soaking in lovely, soft bubbles. Where she could hear the "good" stereo (not Joel's transistor radio that usually needed batteries). And the most amazing thing was that Dad let her go! "But that's not fair!" we'd whine. Nevertheless, she went.

You probably have your own memories of childhood injustices. Big brothers who got their own rooms while you had to share with a little sister. Neighbors who got better allowances and newer bicycles than you did. Kids who were *paid* for their good grades. And you probably raised the same cry that we all did: "It's not fair!"

The response that most parents give (authors included) is something along the lines of "Life's not fair," which is true. But turn to Luke 10:38 and watch how Jesus handled a case of "injustice."

Martha might well be called Martha *Stewart*. When Jesus, an important guest, arrived at her home, she busied herself with preparations. (After all, the goose had to be marinated in herbs from her garden. And certainly Jesus would appreciate the cornhusk and wildberry garland she'd created for the dining room.) While Martha rushed, her sister Mary rested at Jesus' feet, soaking in every word He had to say. Well, like any sister,

Martha complained. "Lord, don't you care that my sister has left me to do the work by myself? Tell her to help me!" In other words, "Jesus, it's not fair! I have to do all the work while she just sits there!" But Jesus didn't say, "Well, life's not fair. Get over it!" He spoke her name, acknowledging her. He understood all that she'd done. "You are worried about many things." Then He redirected her to the thing that was most important at the time—His teachings. To Martha's "It's not fair," Jesus indicated, "It's not important." Jesus showed Martha that justice isn't always what's fair.

Life *is* filled with injustices—from the petty, childish things we've all complained about to heart-wrenching things that make us sadly shake our heads. Let's follow Jesus' example and turn our eyes away from the inequity and focus on Him.

> *Lord Jesus, thank You for the truths*
> *You've shown in Your Word.*
> *Help me to focus on You,*
> *when life seems so unfair.*
> *Help me show my children*
> *that resting at Your feet*
> *is more important than*
> *any justice*
> *we might seek.*

YA GOTTA STAND UP

For those who will fight bravely and not yield,
there is triumphant victory
over all dark things of life.
—James Allen[75]

He has showed you,
O man, what is good.
And what does the Lord require of you?
To act justly and to love mercy
and to walk humbly with your God.
Micah 6:8

Have you ever scanned the newspaper and asked, "Isn't there any *good* news?" Or you flip on the evening news, but after watching the lead stories, turn it off before you get too depressed? Sometimes it seems like the media is full of heartbreaking stories of abuse, pain, lawlessness, and injustice. It's likely that there are days when you can't even take it all in. Most of us just shake our heads, murmur a prayer, then try to forget about it.

But some women are taking action to right the wrongs.

They're on a mission to bring comfort and some sense of relief to those who are hurt. In fact, the victim's rights movement is one of the nation's fastest-growing civil rights movements.[76] Women like Marilyn, who established Abused Deaf Women's Advocacy Services. Marilyn's organization helps deaf women who are the victims of domestic violence and sexual assault.[77] Then there's Yvonne, a woman who devotes her time to Neighbors Who Care, a group of church members who provide moral support and daily living help to victims.[78] Betty and Harriet are two women who worked together to form Justice for Murder Victims, a victim's advocacy group.[79] Although these women live in different communities across the country, they all have something in common. They or someone they knew was a victim of a violent crime. Their lives were touched so dramatically that they had to stand up for justice. They just couldn't sit there.

Each of our lives will be touched by painful injustices. Jobs that are lost unfairly, health problems that are undeserved, and crimes that go unpunished plague our world. Sometimes, justice is beyond our grasp—we simply have to give it to God in prayer. But other times, we *can* act to advocate justice. We can stand up for victims or ones who can't stand on their own. We can help our kids look for solutions and answers. We can show that action *does* get results.

You may not have to form an organization, but you will have to stand up.

> *God, our world is filled with injustice and pain.*
> *Help me seek justice and peace,*
> *while teaching my children to do the same.*

KICK THIS AROUND

*Ten years from now, nobody's going to
be impressed that I was homecoming queen,
but they might think it was cool
I could kick a 40-yard field goal.*
—Katie Hnida [80]

*Now to him who is able to do immeasurably
more than all we ask or imagine,
according to his power that is at work within us,
to him be glory in the church
and in Christ Jesus throughout all generations,
for ever and ever! Amen.*
Ephesians 3:20–21

I t's halftime during the homecoming game for Chatfield High School. Time to crown the homecoming king and queen. The members of the homecoming court stand on the field while the announcer calls out the names of two teenagers. You'd think no one would be surprised that one of these smiling kids is wearing shoulder pads and removes a football helmet to receive the crown.

Except those huge pads sure make the king look so tiny. . . .

Yep. The 1998 homecoming queen for Chatfield High is none other than the football team's attractive placekicker, Katie Hnida (Nye-duh). Who would have thought? Not only is Katie an intelligent and pretty high school senior, at the time of her homecoming game, her kicking was perfect, being 23 for 23 on extra points and 3 for 3 on field goals.

Actually, it's not unheard of for girls to be playing football anymore. In 1998, there were thirty-eight female varsity football players in Colorado alone. But it's still pretty rare.[81]

Some might say, "We've come a long way, baby." Remember when the people racing to put out fires were fire*men*? Or only men were called "cops"? Here are a few historical dates involving women to give a little perspective:

- 1919, the Nineteenth Amendment passes, giving women the right to vote.
- 1972, Bernice Gera was the first female umpire in professional baseball.
- 1983, Sally Ride became the first American woman to travel in space.
- 1996, four women entered the Citadel and survived the physically grueling "hell week."

Yes, there are many that believe women haven't come far enough. But right now let's celebrate the women who have taken those first courageous steps to lead us where we are right now. What kind of bravery did it take for suffragettes to stand up to their fathers, brothers, and husbands as they demanded the right to vote? Imagine the grit and guts it took for the young women fighting to prove themselves at the Citadel. Think of the courage so many women before us have had in applying for schools, jobs, and positions always given to men. They didn't give up when it looked like their dreams were going to be dashed.

Can you be a mother who gives her children courage to make their dreams come true? When your son says, "I'd like to try that!" or your daughter shares, "This is my dream!" do you snicker, "You can't do that! It'll never work! You're not smart enough, not tall enough, not fast enough" or any other "not enough" you can interject? Or do you help your child find a path to make those dreams a reality? And perhaps *you* still have dreams you've left behind. Even if it takes ten years to reach your goal, where will you be in ten years if you don't try?

Lord, let me inspire my children
to reach toward their dreams
by the courageous example I set.

IN THE FACE OF FEAR

You are under the unfortunate delusion that,
simply because you run away from danger,
you have no courage.
You're confusing courage with wisdom.
—The Wizard of Oz[82]

Be strong and courageous. Do not be terrified;
do not be discouraged, for the Lord your God
will be with you wherever you go.
Joshua 1:9

Although the Bible hardly mentions her name, Jochebed was an incredible woman of courage. In a time of persecution, death, and slavery, she showed her children what it meant to fearlessly stand against the enemy.

Imagine her pregnancy—nine agonizing, yet wonderful months of anticipation. According to Pharaoh's order, if her baby were a boy, she would have to throw the infant into the Nile River. Yet if the child were a girl, she would be allowed to live. What unbelievable joy and pain went through Jochebed's mind when she first gazed upon her baby son! Exodus 2:2 tells us that "she saw that he was a fine child." In her heart of hearts, she knew she could never follow Pharaoh's command.

It must have been a tense three months in that household. Picture Jochebed, hurrying to muffle each cry. Nursing in the shadows. Hushing the precious cooing of the tiny baby. Holding her breath each time Pharaoh's army passed by. As the baby grew, so did the tension.

What a courageous woman, to boldly defy a powerful king! To say, "My love for this child is greater than Pharaoh's command." Not only did God use this dauntless woman to carry out His mighty plan, but God used her to raise up another mighty leader. Miriam.

Miriam watched her mother choose love over law. She saw the tears in her mother's eyes as she gently placed the infant in the papyrus basket. Miriam understood what courage was. She saw the importance of a bold heart each time she looked at her tiny baby brother. And Miriam followed her mother's example, stepping out of the rushes to speak with Pharaoh's daughter. Miriam's courageous actions allowed Jochebed to raise Moses openly, with the *blessing* of the king! Many years later, Miriam would become a prophetess and leader among the Israelites.

Although we may not face heartless laws or rulers as Jochebed did, we *are* called to live with courage. And it can be tough!

A young woman in our church recently got up the courage to share her faith with her non-Christian husband. Not only was she frightened that he might reject her, but it was painful for her to realize that he was far from accepting her belief in and love for Christ. As she cried later that week, her six-year-old daughter asked what was wrong. "Your daddy doesn't believe in Jesus. I'm just sad that he won't get to go to heaven," she explained. As this woman shared a simple gospel message, she was able to lead her daughter to the Lord. God used her courage and faithfulness to reach a child in a powerful way.

Perhaps you need the courage to step out of your circle of friends to welcome someone new. Maybe it's hard for you to boldly share your faith in Christ. Or it could be that you just need the heart to stand up to an "enemy" in your life. Just as Jochebed likely discovered—stepping out in faith might not be a cake walk! There will be stresses. You may have to muffle your own cries and silently celebrate victories. But she'd also tell you (a hundred times over!) that it's worth it.

Lord, give me courage today.
I want to show my children
what it means to trust God
in any circumstance.
Help me rely on You
and boldly step out in faith to follow You.

GREAT EXPECTATIONS

But no one except Lucy knew
that as it circled the mast it had whispered to her, "Courage,
dear heart," and the voice,
she felt sure, was Aslan's, and with the voice
a delicious smell breathed in her face.
—C. S. Lewis[83]

I eagerly expect and hope
that I will in no way be ashamed,
but will have sufficient courage so that now as always
Christ will be exalted in my body,
whether by life or by death.
Philippians 1:20

I'm pregnant!"

How exciting to say these words. Some women think of creative ways to break the news to their husbands or families. An extra place set at the table for dinner, with a tiny silver spoon on the plate. A package that, when opened, reveals a newborn's sleeper. A "101 Baby Names" book left on the coffee table.

Whatever the method, there's always excitement when this message of joy is shared.

But what if the message of joy went beyond what is considered "normal"? What if the thrill of discovering you were pregnant also brought the potential for death? We can only imagine what went through the minds of Bobbi and Kenny McCaughey when they learned they were expecting not one, two, or even three babies, but seven. Seven! No woman had ever survived such a pregnancy, nor had all of the babies.

Doctors were certain of the dangers this pregnancy would bring. They immediately suggested that four of the babies be aborted or, as they more delicately put it, the pregnancy should be "selectively reduced." But the McCaugheys refused. "Taking a life is up to God, not us," they responded. These seven growing babies were a gift from God, and they would take them all.

What incredible courage this couple demonstrated. When news of this incredible pregnancy reached the media, the opinions of the world were heard daily. Many thought it foolish to bring this many children into the world. "How will they feed them? How will they send them all to school? How? How?" But Bobbi and Kenny stood firm. They weren't out to please the masses. They were courageous enough to believe in God and trust that He would determine the outcome.

We all know that Bobbi survived the pregnancy and that each of those seven children lived as well. Kenneth, Alexis, Natalie, Kelsey, Nathan, Brandon, and Joel. Add to that big sister Mikayla, and you've got more than a full house. But the McCaugheys have received gifts from all around the world. College tuitions have been promised. A new house has been built. Formula was donated, as well as a fifteen-passenger van. The list goes on and on. God provides.[84]

What a beautiful lesson we learn from this couple. They had the courage to say no to the wisdom of the world and do what was right, no matter what the outcome. Can we say the same for ourselves? Do we sway at the whims of our peers? Do we turn around when the road ahead looks too rough? Are we afraid to say, "This is what I believe, and I will not back down"?

The eight McCaughey children will forever be thankful for the courage of their parents. What about your children? What kind of courage and strength will they learn from you?

Powerful Lord,
You have given me the ability to choose.
Grant me the courage to choose wisely.

WHAT ARE YOU AFRAID OF?

"By golly, no monsters are going to get us tonight!
Wither and die, bloodsucking freaks of nature!"
—Calvin, from Calvin and Hobbes[85]

Even though I walk through the valley of the
shadow of death, I will fear no evil,
for you are with me.
Psalm 23:4

Do you suffer from aichmophobia? If so, you'd better hide the scissors because you're afraid of sharp objects. Or perhaps you have linonophobia and use a lot of tape because you're afraid of string. If you have amathophobia, you probably celebrate Valentine's Day with lots of chocolate since you're afraid of flowers. We suppose folks with trichophobia shave their heads due to the fact that they're afraid of hair. And how do people with cathisophobia drive a car? After all, they're afraid of sitting down![86]

According to The Anxiety Network (yes, a *real* Web site), the word "phobia" comes from the Greek for "fear." There are hundreds of phobias, ranging from geumophobia —fear of flavors—to aulophobia—fear of flutes. Although we may smile and shake our heads, these are actual fears that are very real to those who suffer from them.

Our society has an odd fixation with fear. Movies like *Scream* and *Psycho* (and their sequels) are blockbuster hits. Stephen King thrillers race to the top of the bestseller book list. In October, haunted houses pop up in major cities, inviting patrons to walk through for the fright of a lifetime. Fears, whether real or "safe"—surround us every day. The result? People who are anxious and apprehensive. People who live under a cloak of suspicion and distrust. Is this what you want to be? Is this the way you want your children to live?

God's Word gives us comfort and reassurance of our fears. In 2 Timothy 1:7, Paul writes, "For God did not give us a spirit of timidity, but a spirit of power." God calls us to be courageous, with the confidence that His protective presence is sufficient. Modeling godly courage is a tremendous way to nudge your children into fear-free living. God desires that we live in joy—not fear. After all, His plans for us *do* include good, hope, and prosperity (Jeremiah 29:11). So what do we have to be afraid of?

All-Knowing God, I know
that You want my life to be filled with joy, not fear.
Protect me from the fears that crowd into my mind.
Replace them with Your peace and courage.

A NEW DEFINITION

As they say,
"That which does not kill us makes us stronger."
—Clairee Belcher in *Steel Magnolias* [87]

When they saw the courage of Peter and John. . .
they were astonished.
Acts 4:13

Courage is defined as "mental or moral strength to venture, persevere, and withstand danger, fear, or difficulty." [88] But how do you define courage in everyday terms? What does it look like? How does it speak? Here are just a few women who define courage in our minds.

Last spring, Lisa found out that she has breast cancer. For many young women, this news would stop them cold. But Lisa is facing this disease with courage, determined to win the battle. In the midst of exhausting chemotherapy treatments (and all the side effects), she works diligently and cheerfully as an art director at a Christian publishing company. Though her workload is difficult and her illness is draining, her attitude is determined.

Through a set of heart-wrenching circumstances, Stacey was unable to adopt the little girl from China that had been promised to her. After going through such a painful experience, most of us would have shaken our heads, afraid to try again. But as this book is being written, Stacey is preparing to become a foster parent—a *single* foster parent. Stacey believes that she has love, a faith in God, and a warm home to share with a hurting child. Her courage is selfless and generous.

It would be easy to list the things that Joy can't do. Born with a neurological disease, her arms and legs are useless. But Joy has so much more to offer! She teaches fourth-graders who are developmentally disabled or don't speak English. From her wheelchair, she speaks to children eye to eye. She is tenacious and dogged in her efforts to help her students. And the children love her for it. "She's my favorite teacher," says one student.[89]

These women define courage. They are brave, relentless, and determined. They all face incredible odds, heartache, setbacks, and tears. They are passing on a legacy of courage to their coworkers, children, students, and friends. But they are a shining example of what courage can do.

Father, give me courage to face the challenges
You've prepared for me today.
Use my words and actions
to define courage for others.

YOU CAN'T HIDE
THOSE LYIN' EYES

There are two kinds of truth.
There are real truths and there are made-up truths.
—Washington D.C. Mayor, Marion Barry[90]

The Lord detests lying lips,
but he delights in men who are truthful.
Proverbs 12:22

A *Family Circle* poll asked women to share their thoughts on honesty. Although 79 percent described themselves as "honest in every facet of life," the results might make you think otherwise.

- 65% confessed to some sort of on-the-job "crime," such as taking office supplies
- 25% reported that they've called in sick when they really weren't ill
- 70% said it's okay to tell a "white lie"

- 69% of women with kids under the age of 18 admit that they've involved their child in a lie, such as having their child lie for them
- 54% of women under the age of 45 would not tell a cashier that he or she had undercharged them

And, when asked about the most important elements in marriage, women ranked honesty fourth.[91]

Honesty has taken a nosedive in today's society. Many will tell you that it's okay to lie, as long as it doesn't hurt anyone. In fact, they'll contend, lying may even spare someone's feelings and save a relationship.

The Bible tells a different story. Consider Ananias and Sapphira, early Christians who sold a plot of land and gave the money to the church (Acts 5:1–11). Sounds incredibly selfless . . . except that they claimed to give *all* the money, although they only gave a portion of it. To make themselves appear more generous, Ananias and Sapphira lied. The apostle Peter admonished them, saying, "You have not lied to men but to God." Both Ananias and Sapphira died instantly.

1 Samuel 16:7 says, "Man looks at the outward appearance, but the Lord looks at the heart." On the outside, you may appear truthful and honest. You may even consider yourself "honest in every facet of life," just as the women in the survey. But look at your heart. Look closely. (You can be certain that God is!) What does God see there? Perhaps the years of dishonesty have created quite a collection. Those "little white lies" have certainly stacked up. And they all look the same to God.

Take a moment to read aloud Psalm 51:10. Then, when faced with the temptation to "stretch the truth," determine to keep your heart pure before God.

Gracious Father, forgive me for the times
when I have been dishonest.
Create in me a pure heart
and give me the strength to keep it that way.

FACE THE MUSIC

Truth does not blush.
—Tertullian[92]

But everything exposed by the light
becomes visible,
for it is light that makes everything visible.
Ephesians 5:13–14

I was a typical snoopy little sister," admits Jody. "Since I was at home when my brother and sisters were at school, I managed to explore their rooms and get into all kinds of trouble."

One afternoon, Jody slipped into Jill's room to check out the toys that would eventually be hers (as the fourth of five children, Jody already knew what hand-me-downs were). Jill's Raggedy Ann doll was lying on the bed. "To this day, I'm not sure what prompted me to do what came next," says Jody. At any rate, she found her brother's fake vampire blood (another "no-no") and used it to "draw" all over poor Raggedy Ann's face. "I remember holding the 'bleeding' doll, thinking, 'Someone's going to see this. I'd better hide it.' " So Jody turned the doll face down on the pillow and left the scene of the crime.

Our dad was also the victim of Jody's afternoon explorations. We all knew that he kept a pack of Wrigley's Doublemint Gum in his desk drawer. Chalk it up to budding creativity, but Jody opened the package, licked off the sugary coating, and made a row of teeth marks on each stick of gum. Then she neatly rewrapped each stick and placed the package back in the drawer, certain that no one would find out.

Well, as the saying goes, the truth *will* find you out. Jill came home and turned over her doll to find a gory mess. (Plus, Joel discovered that his fake vampire blood was missing, and Mom wasn't too happy to find that one of her nice pillowcases was ruined.) Dad came home to enjoy a stick of gum and discovered a preschool art project instead. In both cases, the truth couldn't be hidden very long. It eventually came to light and consequences were felt by many family members.

The truth will always come to light. Max Lucado writes, "The ripple of today's lie is tomorrow's wave and next year's flood."[93] Our dishonesty, whether it is discovered today or far into the future, has impact on our lives and on the lives of those we love. Hearts are stained with mistrust. Confidence is marred.

There's a story about a man who conned his way into the orchestra of the emperor of China. Though the man had no musical talent, he faked his way through each practice, simply holding the flute in place and moving his fingers while the other musicians played. Because of his deception, he was paid well and lived comfortably.

Then the emperor requested a solo from each musician. The flutist panicked and pretended to be sick. Unfortunately, the royal physician wasn't fooled. When the day came for the flutist to play his solo, he took poison and killed himself. This incident led to a phrase that we've all used: "He refused to face the music."[94]

The Bible speaks repeatedly of men and women who tried to hide the truth. Adam and Eve. Cain. Achan. David. Haman. (And that's just the Old Testament!) Their deceit was uncovered and the effects were felt generations after them.

When you're tempted to be dishonest, have the courage to face the music. No lie ever glorified God. And no lie has ever remained in the dark for long.

Gracious Father, give me the courage to be honest.
Help me to face the music
so my children will know the consequences of truth
rather than deceit.

TO TELL THE TRUTH

Remember girls, we hide our flaws
until after the wedding!
—Cinderella's stepmother[95]

Surely you desire truth in the inner parts;
you teach me wisdom in the inmost place.
Psalm 51:6

Have you ever met someone and thought, "I'd like to be her friend," right away? Or, on the other hand, met someone and thought, "We'll never get along!" Amy had the latter thought when she first met Ellen. Here's how Amy remembers their meeting:

"My husband, Mike, and Ellen's husband, Rick, had become friends at work. Since we both had boys the same age, they thought our families might become friends as well and arranged for us to have dinner at Rick and Ellen's.

"Ellen graciously welcomed us into their home. She was thin, had great hair, prepared a delicious dinner, and to top it all, their apartment was spotless. And when we learned they'd had a birthday party for their son just a couple hours earlier yet still managed to have their home so clean, that was just the last straw. I thought, 'I'll never be able to be friends with this woman—she's too perfect!'

"Later in the evening I needed to nurse our son. I asked where I could go for a bit of privacy. Ellen faltered a second, then pointed to a closed door. 'You can use our room,' she offered.

"I opened the door. The room was a disaster! Toys, wrapping paper, balloons, and all kinds of leftovers from the birthday party were stacked and strewn all around. And my first thought was, 'I have a new friend!' Sure enough, more than eight years have passed and Ellen remains one of my dearest friends. She's still thin, still has great hair, and actually does keep her house much cleaner than mine, but I know she's not completely perfect. That lets me open up and be more honest with her myself—I don't feel like she's judging me from her throne of perfection."

Do you have trouble letting people see your flaws? You may be a woman who primps in front of the mirror for hours before leaving the house—don't want anyone to see you without your hair curled or your makeup just right! Or you might be one who never opens the door to guests unless the rooms are immaculate and vases of fresh flowers grace the tables. Yet, try as you might, underneath it all, you're still imperfect. We all are.

There's nothing wrong with wanting to put your best foot forward, just as Ellen did by quickly cleaning the main rooms of her home. But when hiding our flaws stands in the way of serving God, friendship, being a great mom, or anything else of importance, it's time to, like Ellen, open the doors and let honesty shine forth. Being dishonest about your defects might be keeping you from some of the greatest joys and rewards in life.

As you think of passing honesty on to your children, evaluate how honest you are about yourself with your children and others. Will your kids grow up thinking only the perfect are acceptable?

God, You know me as I am and still love me.
Help me to stop finding flaws with myself
and let others love me for who I truly am as well.

DRIVING HOME THE TRUTH

Our first line of defense
in raising children with values is
modeling good behavior ourselves.
—Fred Gosman[96]

The integrity of the upright guides them,
but the unfaithful are destroyed by their duplicity.
Proverbs 11:3

School mornings are undeniably hectic for most of us. The same kids who could have outrun an Olympian last night, have suddenly developed a case of lead feet. Clothes that looked fine last night apparently wrinkled while you slept. And all at once, children remember vitally important information—like the fact that you were supposed to bake and decorate six dozen cupcakes for today's school party. So perhaps we shouldn't be too hard on the woman in the following story.

It seems that Sarah's morning was a little rushed, to say the least. In a desperate hurry to get her two daughters to school, she found herself in the middle of a traffic jam when she should

191

have been pulling into the school parking lot. Now, most of us are familiar with the frustration of traffic jams—that endless line of unmoving cars that seems to lurk around every bend, especially when we're running late. So maybe you can understand what Sarah did next.

In an effort to get around the traffic jam, she drove up onto the sidewalk and across people's yards. A female police officer, who was trying to direct traffic, demanded that she stop. Then the officer leaned into the car to talk to Sarah. Apparently that was the proverbial straw that broke the camel's back, because Sarah declared that she didn't have time for this. . .then she hit the gas. That would have been bad enough, but her rotten morning was about to get worse. When the officer had leaned into the car, her arm had become tangled in the seat belt. So when Sarah drove off in a rage, the officer was dragged about ten feet. Another officer followed Sarah down the road at about 75 mph, before Sarah pulled up in front of the school.[97]

Obviously, Sarah will have to face some serious legal consequences of her actions. But she'll also have to face the moral consequences. All this action took place in front of her two children, ages ten and thirteen. What did Sarah's actions say to her daughters? What did they take away from the situation? Maybe they'll remember it as a wild adventure on the way to school. But Sarah's attitude speaks loudly. "It's okay to bend the rules as long as you don't get caught." Her lack of integrity put on a show that morning and will likely leave a lasting impression on her girls.

Things *do* get hectic for us. There are days when we *don't* have time for life's frustrations. Often, it's easy to "bend the rules" or "tell a white lie" in order to avoid certain consequences. Perhaps a better response is to take a deep breath and be honest. Rather than becoming entangled in lies or running away from the consequences, let your integrity do the driving. Even on school mornings!

Gracious Lord, keep my eyes on You today
so that my actions and words will be rich with honesty.
In moments of stress or frustration,
I turn my heart over to You.
Guide my footsteps today
that they may walk in a straight path
that my children may follow.

BIBLE BIBS

I hate housework!
You make the beds, you do the dishes—
and six months later you have to start all over again.
—Joan Rivers[98]

I have hidden your word in my heart
that I might not sin against you.
Psalm 119:11

Amy spoke to a group of mothers recently and was describing the creative ways her family entertains themselves by inventing obstacle courses out of couch cushions (don't step in the hot lava!), throwing footballs through cardboard rings hung from the ceiling, or shooting suction darts at targets drawn on the windows with a bar of soap.

One mother gasped and loudly interrupted, "Your house must be a sty!"

Well, not quite a sty, but Amy is quick to admit she's "cleaning challenged." In fact, not long ago Jody gave her a book called *Polish Your Furniture with Panty Hose.* Here we both gleaned such cleaning tips as these:

- Bounce dryer sheets can be used to collect cat hair. Of course, neither of us has cats, but that's beside the point!
- You can wash dishes with Clairol Herbal Essence shampoo.
- A can of Coca-Cola, poured into a toilet bowl and left for an hour, can rinse away stains.
- Colgate toothpaste is great for cleaning piano keys, removing crayon from walls, and polishing the silver.
- Furniture reflects with brilliant sheen when buffed with SPAM. (You might want to think twice about this cleaning method if you have dogs who like to chew.)[99]

We both got some good laughs out of this book, but Amy never took the message to heart and still has dust on her piano and yesterday's dishes stacked in the sink. She thinks there are things more important than a clean house. Like laughter. Like time to cuddle and read with a toddler. Like a clean heart.

You may nag and pester your children to keep their rooms clean. Or perhaps you've passed on to them your "clean genes" and they automatically make their beds and offer to fold the laundry. Have you passed on to them the importance of keeping their hearts clean? You most likely put a bib on your children when they were young to protect their clean clothes from stains. Now it's time to teach them, by your example, to protect their hearts from the stain of sin.

We thank God for His incredible forgiveness. He never has a laundry problem since He can wash away the sin from the dirtiest heart. Yet just as we know it's best to protect a child's clothes with a bib, it's best to protect our hearts with Scripture. The less we sin, the less we must ask forgiveness from God, our husbands, our children, our coworkers, our neighbors, our friends. . .my the list does go on!

Open your Bible and notice the verses you've underlined over the years. What verses have encouraged you? Which ones have lifted your spirits during dark hours? Which passages have taught you of God's incredible love? Choose a few of these and begin to memorize them. We suggest you start with Psalm 119:11. Write these verses on cards and tape them inside the kitchen cabinets. Input them as screen-savers on your computer. Paint them with eyeliner on your bathroom mirror. Get your whole family involved in hiding God's messages in their hearts as protection against the stain of sin.

Forgiving Father, help me
to recall Your words of guidance
when I'm tempted to sin.

A CHAMPION
FOR CHASTITY

He is pushing you,
you have to choose. . .
don't confuse what love is,
with what some say
love should be.
—Michael W. Smith[100]

Do not share in the sins of others.
Keep yourself pure.
1 Timothy 5:22

To Esther Splaine, they are simply "her girls." But these eleven teenagers meet with Esther for more than "girl talk." They're members of Girls Against Premarital Sex, a support group for teens who want to remain abstinent until marriage. Once a week, Esther gathers her girls to discuss strategies for dealing with boyfriends who want to have sex. They engage in role-playing sessions to help them practice ways to say "No." They talk about the lines they've heard and the struggles they've had. Most of all, these young women realize that they're not alone in their pursuit of purity.

"I tell my girls to call me any time, twenty-four hours a day, if they need help. I've got five kids of my own. What's eleven more?" Esther smiles.[101] She also requires that group members attend a church, temple, or mosque weekly or join a religious youth group. In a culture that generally accepts teen sexual activity, Esther is giving her girls the courage and confidence to stand up for virtue. Often, it may seem like a losing battle. But to Esther, it's worth it.

"These girls have the same dreams other girls have—they dream of getting married, having babies, and living in a nice house. Sex before marriage has a way of taking all that away."

Esther is giving her girls more than an opportunity to fulfill their dreams. She's weaving a support system—a safety net—that girls can rely on when the pressure gets tough. She's giving them the skills and the voice to tell others that purity *is* important. And she's standing up for morality when other adults would rather turn away.

Often we're embarrassed or unsure how to handle the issue of purity. So we mumble a few awkward phrases or don't say anything at all. But if you don't say something, you can bet that someone else will. . .and it's likely that person won't share your values. Take a cue from Esther. Be open about sexual purity. Offer realistic solutions to tough situations. Encourage kids to get involved in church activities. Be a champion for chastity (you may be the only one your kids see).

198

Make it clear that your kids can call on you twenty-four hours a day. Most importantly, give them a passion for purity.

Loving God, I lift up my children to You.
They face so many moral battles each day.
Strengthen them and give them wisdom.
Let me instill in them a passion for purity
that their lives may glorify You in every way.

THE CURE

The heat of passion for a moment
Could burn you for a lifetime to come.
One minute's pleasure might put off your pain
But it takes the innocence from the young.
—Wayne Watson[102]

For I am the Lord, who heals you.
Exodus 15:26

In its heyday, smallpox marched across the world, infecting ten to fifteen million people *every year.* Approximately two million of those infected would die.[103] Those who didn't die were likely to be left with permanent, unsightly scars covering their body. The disease took the lives of children, adults, teens, and the elderly. It seemed that no one was safe. You see, smallpox is a virus, which means "poison."[104] Alone, it is relatively harmless—but once it finds a living host, this poison replicates again and again and again, until it harms or completely destroys its host.

Although there is still no *cure* for smallpox, there is a

solution. In the 1960s, scientists discovered an amazingly simple and wonderful vaccine, which can prevent smallpox infection. In 1967, the UN World Health Or-ganization originated a worldwide vaccination program against smallpox. By 1979, smallpox had essentially disappeared from the earth.

A similar "disease" is marching across our world today. Some call it promiscuity, others refer to it as loose morals, or "high-risk" behavior. God simply calls it sin and its effects are very real. According to George Barna, cohabitation has risen by more than 500 percent in the past two decades. One of three children born this year will be born to an unwed mother.[105] Another study revealed that almost half of the nation's students are sexually active—seven percent *before* the age of thirteen. The same study determined that an alarming number of young people "experiment with risky behaviors."[106] Sexual sin destroys lives and leaves its victims scarred. So how do you prevent your children from this epidemic?

The vaccine isn't as simple as a shot in the arm. It requires honesty—talking openly with kids about sexuality and sexual sin *before* you think they might be "infected." It requires boldness—there is nothing shameful about purity, yet we put off "The Talk" with embarrassment. Most of all, keeping your kids from the epidemic of sexual sin requires prayer. You can't control their thoughts and actions, but you *can* place your kids in the hands of a faithful and powerful God.

We immunize our children from measles, mumps, chickenpox, and tetanus. We use antibacterial soap, bleach, and hot water. We scrub their hands, wipe their noses, and tell them to cover their mouths when they cough. Why not treat the virus—the poison—of sexual sin the same way?

Mighty God, our world is infected
with the poison of sin.
Protect us from this disease and give me
the wisdom to help my children remain pure.
May they be shining examples of
godliness in a fallen world.

HANG IN THERE!

Stand firm for what you know is right
It's wise, as I have found
The mighty oak was once a nut
That simply held its ground.
—Agnes W. Thomas[107]

I will strengthen you and help you;
I will uphold you with my righteous right hand.
Isaiah 41:10

You might say that the Ayala sisters like to hang around together—literally. Alexis, Andrea, and Michelle are fifth-generation performers with Ringling Brothers and Barnum & Bailey's Circus. Their talent? Hair suspension.

Before each performance, the sisters braid special ropes with steel buckles into their waist-length hair. Then they attach a steel cord to their braided buns and are gently hoisted thirty feet above the arena—without safety nets or harnesses! With only their tresses to hold them up, the young women present a series of graceful spins and juggling tricks. "It hurts, but we don't think about the pain when we are performing," says Alexis.[108]

Although your children probably don't make a living dangling thirty feet above the ground, they do face awesome challenges every day. Among those challenges is the commitment to remain sexually pure until marriage. Most often, young adults will face this task without the safety net of your presence. While peer pressure tugs at their morals, society pulls their ideals in a different direction, and kids frantically juggle everything from hormones to beliefs.

Just as the Ayala sisters braid strong cords into their hair, you can weave strength and determination into your child's character. When things like open communication, a godly example, and lots of prayer intertwine, the result is a sturdy character that can withstand pressure. Your child's view of purity will be tested at one time or another. Begin weaving the cords that will help them hang in there.

Wise God, thank You for my children.
I pray that Your love and my love
may intertwine to strengthen them
in the trials ahead.

SPILLED MILK?

Someday He'll call us and we will
come running and fall in His arms
and the tears will fall down and we'll pray,
"I want to fall in love with You,
my heart beats for You."
—Dan Haseltine[109]

Blessed are the pure in heart,
for they will see God.
Matthew 5:8

Y ou're having a brunch for a group of ladies from church. There are flowers in lovely vases about the room. The table is set with your nicest white, linen tablecloth. And just before the women arrive, you bring out a beautiful pitcher, fill it with hot black coffee, and place it on the table. The doorbell rings, and as you turn to answer it, you trip over the edge of a rug and bump the pitcher. With a hot splash, coffee spills over the edge of the pitcher and onto the tablecloth. What's left to do but mop it up and try to cover the spot with a plate of muffins?

It's a fact of life. If the pitcher gets bumped, the contents will spill out. If punch is inside, punch comes out. If the pitcher is filled with milk, that's what gets spilled. No matter how pretty the pitcher is on the outside, it's the contents that over-flow in a crisis. Pretty basic information. You don't even need a degree in physics to figure this one out. Whatever is inside will come out.

You know, the same thing is true with us. Whatever is inside of us will spill out when we get bumped. No matter how attractive we are or how spiritual we appear, it's what's inside that counts. For example, you listen to coworkers swear and complain with foul words. Their language begins to fill your mind, yet you think nothing of it. Then you shut your thumb in your desk drawer, and out comes a string of profanities. Where did that come from?

It's back to that old saying, "Garbage In, Garbage Out." Whatever we put into our hearts and minds is what will later come pouring out. It's time to consider what we allow our eyes to see, our ears to hear, and our minds to savor. Take time now to evaluate what you're filling up on.

Philippians 4:8 tells us, "Whatever is true, whatever is noble, whatever is right, whatever is pure, whatever is lovely, whatever is admirable—if anything is excellent or praise-worthy—think about such things." Hold this measure up to what is filling the pitcher of your heart. Are you filling your heart with things that are pure? True? Noble? Consider the books you read, the music you listen to, the movies and televi-sion shows you watch, and the friends you choose. How do they stand up against this verse?

The course of our lives is unsure. We don't know if tomorrow we'll be on vacation in Europe or in the hospital with a raging disease. We can hope for smooth sailing, but it's more likely we'll have rough and stormy seas to deal with in the days ahead. How will we respond when the road is full of potholes instead of fresh pavement?

Last year Amy and her family were in the process of adopting a baby. For months they purchased baby clothes, hunted for cribs, debated over names, and so on. But the road curved where they thought it would go straight. The birth mother decided to keep her baby. According to the analogy, their pitcher got bumped. Amy shares, "Yes, we were sad—even heartbroken. But we still could love this young woman and not lash out at her in hate. This wasn't because we're so wonderful and have incredible control of our emotions. Instead, it was because we had filled our hearts with God's love, and that's what was still in our hearts when the situation changed."

When a cup of hot coffee is spilled, the liquid can be washed away, but you can forever burn the minds of those you love with the heat of your anger. A spilled pitcher of punch may stain your tablecloth, but that can later be bleached. Bitter words can stain the hearts of your children forever. Because when you're bumped, whatever is inside will come spilling out.

Keep your heart pure.

Lord, as did the psalmist, we ask of You,
"Create in me a pure heart, O God."

AIR PRESSURE

You are the wind beneath my wings.
—sung by Bette Midler[110]

But those who hope in the Lord
will renew their strength.
They will soar on wings like eagles;
they will run and not grow weary,
they will walk and not be faint.
Isaiah 40:31

Okay, it's science experiment time. Yes, that means you. Come on, it's an easy one!

Get out your blow-dryer and a lightweight ball. A small beach ball, a balloon, or even a paper wad will work. Now turn on the blow-dryer (you can leave it on the "cool" setting so you don't get burned) and point the stream of air toward the ceiling. Gently set the ball in the stream of air and let go. It floats! It bounces! It doesn't fall down!

Impress your kids (friends, neighbors, the mail carrier) with this cool stunt and soon you'll be more popular than Bill

Nye the Science Guy!

So how does it work? This is called the Bernoulli effect, named after Daniel Bernoulli, who back in the 1700s discovered basic principles of fluids and aerodynamics. Moving air causes a change of pressure. The pressure within the airstream is less than the pressure outside the airstream. That means the greater outside pressure pushes the ball in on all sides, leaving it balanced in the airstream. This principle is involved in explaining how heavy airplanes can fly (but don't ask us to get that technical—this is about as scientific as we get!). [111]

This fun experiment has great application for our lives. Let's say God is the airstream and we're the balloon. God applies pressure on us that lifts us and supports us. The pressures of the world are all about us, trying to knock us this way and that. These pressures are strong and can be frightening. But as long as we leave the airstream on, God carries us along.

Now, in our science experiment, the only way for the balloon to leave the airstream is to turn off the air. It's the same with God and us. God is as constant as the airstream. But when we consciously turn off the airstream by avoiding time with God, leaving our Bibles to gather dust, closing our hearts to God's voice, we are suddenly unsupported and quickly fall into the abyss of the world. Of course, in reality, God hasn't gone anywhere. We're the ones who have moved ourselves out of His presence.

God, as air, is invisible. In fact, this science project is a great object lesson for teaching your kids about faith in God. Just as air has the power to support an airplane, God has the power to support us. We've just got to stay in the airstream.

> *Powerful God, when the pressures of the world*
> *are squeezing about me,*
> *let me feel Your gentle hands*
> *supporting me and guiding me.*

OH, THE WONDER
OF IT ALL!

Then sings my soul,
my Savior God, to Thee.
How great Thou art,
how great Thou art.
—Stuart K. Hine[112]

God saw all that he had made,
and it was very good.
Genesis 1:31

Share these amazing facts with your kids to help them understand the wonder of God's creation. Then celebrate the creative and ingenious God we serve!

Man may have invented thermos bottles, but God came up with the concept when He created the praying mantis. The praying mantis makes insulated coverings to protect her eggs from the weather. After laying eggs, the mantis surrounds them with foamy bubbles that work on the same principle as a thermos bottle. The temperature outside may be bitterly cold or burning hot, but the eggs will be protected at a safe, constant temperature.

Thomas Edison may have invented the telephone, but the idea has been around ever since God made spiders. The orb weaver spider attaches a "telephone line" to the center of her web, then pulls it tight. The spider brings the line to her hiding place, where she sleeps. The second an insect touches the web, the line vibrates, awakening the spider. The spider crosses the "telephone line," sort of like a bridge to the center of the web, and then moves to the entangled insect.

Think air conditioning is a modern convenience? Nope! God thought up that one for the honeybee. Honeybees keep a constant temperature and a specific condition of airflow so their larvae (or babies) will develop properly and the honey will be suitably cured. Some bees—called fanners—hold themselves to the bottom of the beehive and quiver their wings at the perfect speed to create and maintain the precise amount of air circulation needed.

Do things go haywire at your house when the refrigerator is on the blink? God provided a way for spiders and some wasps to have fresh food, without refrigerators or ice. Since spiders need live meat to survive, and they can't always catch enough for one day, God equipped them with a special liquid. Spiders inject their prey with this liquid, which stuns and immobilizes the insects, but does not kill them. Wasps are supplied with a similar solution in order to preserve caterpillars and spiders that they feed their babies.[113]

In Luke 12:24, Jesus reminds us, "Consider the ravens:

They do not sow or reap, they have no storeroom or barn; yet God feeds them. And how much more valuable you are than birds!" Not only do we serve a mighty and powerful God, but a God who cares and provides for His creation.

Loving God, I praise You for Your majesty,
Your creativity, and Your provision.
What an amazing world You've given me,
filled with examples of Your power.
Thank You for caring for me
and providing the ultimate sacrifice
that I may live forever with You.

BECAUSE I SAID SO

The answer, my friend, is blowin' in the wind,
The answer is blowin' in the wind.
—Bob Dylan[114]

Will the one who contends with
the Almighty correct him?
Job 40:2

Here are some deep questions we found floating around on the Internet. Take time to consider:

- If a cow laughed, would milk come out her nose?
- What's the speed of dark?
- Why is "abbreviated" such a long word?
- Why do banks charge you a "nonsufficient funds fee" on money they already know you don't have?
- Why is a carrot more orange than an orange?
- Why does bottled lemon juice contain

mostly artificial ingredients, but dish-
washing liquid contains real lemon?
- Why are there five syllables in the word
"monosyllabic"?
- Why do they call it the Department of
Interior when they're in charge of everything outdoors?

Reading through these may make you laugh, and it may remind you of being the mother of a preschooler who hears the continuous refrain of "Why? How come? Why?"

It's likely you've already been asked to explain how the stars hang in the sky, what happens to worms when they die, and why it rains. And sometimes your answers, no matter how age-appropriate you make them, just aren't enough. "But why? How?" The questions keep coming. And in exasperation, you give that brilliant answer, "Because I said so!" and mentally ask a question of your own, "Why me?"

This brings to mind a question-asker from the Bible—Job. Here was a wealthy man, content with his family and faithful to God. He is put to the test (to put it mildly) and loses everything. His children and servants are killed, his livestock are stolen or killed, and his body is infected with painful sores. Then his wife starts mocking him and his friends show up to endlessly discuss Job's faults.

Job has his ups and downs through this series of events, but steadfastly refuses to curse God. He does, however, want one thing—to ask God "Why?"

God doesn't do what we expect. He doesn't cuddle Job

in His lap and say, "Let me explain a few things." He doesn't share Job's tears saying, "Yeah, the world's a harsh place." Instead, God answers with a few questions of His own. "Have you ever given orders to the morning? Does the rain have a father? Do you know the laws of heaven? Does the eagle soar at your command?" In essence, God says, "Job, I am so much bigger and more powerful than you can begin to imagine. Who are you to question Me?"

Job quickly backs off, answering, "I spoke of things I did not understand."

How true.

Our children badger us with questions, yet we have questions of our own. Why is there evil in the world? Why didn't God give mothers as much energy as their kids? How can I gather enough patience to get through this day?

Like Job, there is much of life we don't understand. And we must sometimes accept God's answer, "Because I said so."

God of Power and Knowledge,
grant me the bit of wisdom I need
to place my trust in You.

FIRST THINGS FIRST

King of my life I crown you now.
You're the ruler of my heart.
I will wear it loud.
—sung by Crystal Lewis[115]

In the morning, O Lord,
you hear my voice;
in the morning I lay
my requests before you
and wait in expectation.
Psalm 5:3

Okay, it's time for another little activity. Rinse the last of the mayo out of the jar, then dig through the cupboard for some uncooked rice. Now you'll need about four walnuts, still in their shells. (If you can't find walnuts, a few golf balls or Ping-Pong balls will work just as well.)

Drop the walnuts into the jar, then pour the rice over the top, filling the jar to the rim. Be sure to shake the contents down good and tight. Now, pour the contents of the jar into a bowl.

Start the activity again, this time, pouring the rice from the bowl into the jar *first*. Then place the walnuts in the jar. What did you notice? The walnuts won't fit. You can push and maneuver them as much as you want, but they won't budge. (And cracking them doesn't count!) In order for it all to fit, the walnuts *must* go first.

Think of the rice as the things we pack into our day. Work, family, cleaning, exercise, meetings, obligations, laundry, cooking, social functions, community activities. . .and the list goes on. Too often, we fill our life with so many "little things," that we don't leave room for the most important thing of all—our relationship with God. We find ourselves sleepily mumbling a quick prayer before bed. Or squeezing in a speedy devotion after dinner and before soccer practice. Think of it this way: Do your kids watch as you frantically cram your faith into each day at the last minute? Or do they see your faith as a starting point—a basis for each day to begin? To truly live for God, we need to put Him into each day *first*.

Once more, empty the contents of the jar into the bowl. Now, place the walnuts in the jar first. As you do, think of ways to show that God comes first in your day. Perhaps you'll start your mornings with a time of prayer or praise. Or set aside some time first thing each day for Bible reading and faith-building. (And be sure to include your kids whenever you can!) Next, pour the rice over the walnuts. You'll be amazed how those "important" things will somehow all fit in, too! Finally, screw a lid on the jar and tighten it. Place the jar somewhere where you (and your family) can't miss it. Use the jar as a reminder to turn to God first, and let the rest of the details fall where they may.

Heavenly Father, You are the first
and most important thing in my life today.
I trust that You'll take care
of all the other things I need to accomplish.

OFF THE WALL

Peace of mind is shuffling slippers
when you call your momma at night.
—Pat Brady[116]

I have set the Lord always before me.
Because he is at my right hand, I will not be shaken.
Psalm 16:8

It had started as an adventure for father and son. They had gone to a climbing wall to test their skills and their daring. The father had climbed the wall without too much difficulty, then rappelled down. Next the son, around the age of ten, was carefully strapped into a harness, helmeted, and given a few last words of instruction. He nimbly climbed one of the difficult rock trails, straight up for fifty feet until he reached the top. Dad and the climbing wall instructors whooped calls of enthusiasm and praise for the boy's agility and bravery. All that was left was for the boy to let go of the rocks on the wall and rappel down to the ground. All that was left. . .

Letting go of your hold, however precarious it may be, to

trust your harness, the ropes, and those holding them, can be just as much a challenge to one's mettle as the actual climbing. At least while you're climbing you have some control as to where your feet are placed, where you'll reach next with your hand. But when you let go, well, it's all up to others at that point. They have to hold the ropes that keep you from falling. Will they be strong enough? What if they let a rope slip? What if? What if?

And so it was with this young boy. He reached the top without a hitch, but when he looked over his shoulder and saw how far he was from the ground, there was no way he was letting go.

His father called words of encouragement from the ground. "It's okay! The ropes can hold you! The instructors won't let you fall! You can do it!"

Still the boy held fast.

The father soon became frustrated, perhaps even embarrassed at his son's lack of courage. "Just let go! Come on! We don't have all day!" His voice was tinged with a hint of anger.

The boy, frustrated, embarrassed, and starting to feel angry himself, began to cry. Still he clung to the wall.

The father had had enough. "For crying out loud, LET GO! I can't believe you're such a sissy!"

As the father continued his tirade below, one of the climbing instructors decided to take different action. She realized the boy would never let go under these conditions. She ran behind the wall and climbed up a service ladder and onto a narrow ledge behind the top of the wall. From there she could look over the wall, place her hands on the boy's, and look into his teary eyes.

"I'm holding you now," she quietly said. "You can relax."

"I'm scared!"

"I know. It is a long way down. But you can do it. I'll help you."

"Can I climb over the top and come down with you?" the boy pleaded.

"No, it wouldn't be safe. The ropes wouldn't be able to hold you back here. You're safer where you are. Can you let go by yourself?"

"No, I can't do it."

"Then I'll help you."

The instructor held onto the boy's hands and wrists until he'd stopped crying and was calm again. Then he let go of one rock and held onto her hand. She held him steady. He let go of the other rock and held onto her hand. She still held strong.

"I'm going to slowly let go of you. As I do, you'll feel the ropes pulling strong around your harness. Can you feel it?"

The boy nodded, and slowly, gently, was released. Within seconds he had been guided safely to the ground, into the relieved embrace of his father.

Amy was that climbing instructor. She knew how hard it was for the boy to let go because she'd been there herself. She knew she could trust the other instructor, her friend. She knew these ropes could support the weight of a car (so they certainly could hold her!). Yet as she was completing her certification to be an instructor, it was hard even for her to let go of the wall and fall back.

It can be hard to trust God. However precarious our situation is, we feel that as long as we have some tiny semblance of control, we're safe. We don't want to lean back, let go, and test the strength of God's hand. But we must. The only other option is to spend the rest of our lives clinging to miniscule rocks until we become exhausted and angry from the strain.

Only then can we look into the faces of our children, hold their hands, and say, "I know how hard it is. But I can't do this for you. You have to let go and trust God yourself."

Faithful Father, Hold me in Your hands of strength.
Look into my eyes and give me courage
to have faith in You.
Only You can keep me from falling.

A LIVING DEFINITION

Can they see God for who He really is,
In what they see in you and me?
—Steven Curtis Chapman[117]

You are like whitewashed tombs,
which look beautiful on the outside
but on the inside are full of
dead men's bones and everything unclean.
In the same way, on the outside you appear
to people as righteous but on the inside
you are full of hypocrisy and wickedness.
Matthew 23:27–28

A visit to the Denver Public Library found these interesting titles. . .and authors:

> *My Friends, the New Guinea Headhunters* by Benjamin T. Butcher
> *Some Reflections on Genius, and Other Essays* by Sir Walter Russell Brain

Death in Early America by Margaret Coffin
Never Too Old by Esther E. Twente
Marryers by Irving Addison Bacheller
Fish, the Great Potential Food Supply by D.B. Finn
Cactus Culture by Ellen Schulz Quillen
Thunder Gods Gold! by Barry Storm
Black, Black, Beautiful Black by Rose Blue
How to Raise Money by Charles W. Gamble[118]

Most of these titles wouldn't raise an eyebrow if they'd been written by an author with a different name. But the coincidence makes us chuckle.

Does your name make people chuckle? I don't mean your given name, like Cathy or Christine, but your *true* name. . . Christian. Is there a connection—or a disconnection—between who you are and what you do? If you were to title the story of your life, would it seem odd to say, "written by a Christian"?

Every day, in everything you do, you're showing your children what it means to be a follower of Christ. You are shaping their definition of the term "Christian." What will that definition include?

Jody's husband, Erik, recalls this story about his mother. "Every morning while we got ready for school, my mom listened to an evangelical radio program. One morning, the program featured a speaker named Larry Bird. My younger brother asked if it was "the" Larry Bird—from the Boston Celtics—who was speaking. Erik said, "No way. You can't be a Christian and a professional athlete." My mom jumped in immediately. "Of course you can! You can be a Christian in whatever you do."

A young woman we've known for years speaks of her parents, who struggled with marital problems for over ten years. "My mom would never agree to a divorce. She just felt like it wasn't what God wanted her to do." As a result of her mother's faith (and God's grace), her parents are happily married today, in spite of amazing odds.

As a Christian, you are a living, walking, breathing definition of Christ to your children. Will you fail in that role? Of course! But Hebrews 12:2 urges us to "fix our eyes on Jesus, the author and perfecter of our faith." Keep your eyes on Jesus. He's not quite done with your chapter yet!

Jesus, help me to be a true definition of You today.
Give me Your patience, Your insight,
Your wisdom, and Your mercy
to show to my children.
I want them to know You
and see You through my life.

HARLOT TO HERO

There is a wild imagination
at work in ordinary lives.
God has a wild imagination.
Come and see, come and be surprised.
—sung by Scott Krippayne[119]

Now faith is being sure of what
we hope for and certain of what we do not see.
This is what the ancients were commended for.
Hebrews 11:1–2

Open your Bible to Hebrews chapter 11. Here are listed some of the great heroes of the Bible. Heroes of the faith.

The list starts with Abel, son of Adam and Eve, who is called a righteous man of faith. Then we read of Enoch, whose faith had pleased God so much that Enoch didn't experience death. In Genesis 5:24 we read that he simply "was no more, because God took him away."

The list continues with Noah, Abraham, Isaac, Jacob, Joseph, the parents of Moses, then Moses himself. Certainly you remember the great faith of these heroes who talked to God, obeyed God, and followed God's desires. From Noah with his massive ark to Moses and the parting of the Red Sea. We cannot deny the faith of these.

Then we read Hebrews 11:31: "By faith the prostitute Rahab, because she welcomed the spies, was not killed with those who were disobedient."

Rahab? The prostitute? A hero of the faith? In fact, the only woman specifically named on this list? Sure, Sarah gets a fleeting reference by being married to Abraham, and Moses' mother is surely included in the term "parents," but Rahab gets the distinction of being the only woman definitely named as a hero of the faith.

Let's review what Rahab did. In Joshua chapter 2, we learn that two spies were sent to Jericho to look over the land. Jericho was the first place the Israelites would conquer in the land God had promised. So this mission of espionage began.

The spies went to the house of Rahab. Perhaps they thought that by going into this "house of ill repute" they wouldn't be noticed. Or they may have chosen Rahab's house because it was on the city wall. Either way, they were still there when the king of Jericho sent his men looking for the spies. Rahab hid the spies on her roof under stalks of flax and sent the king's men on their way. She committed treason! Then she asked the spies to spare her life and the lives of her family members in exchange for risking her life.

This is a daring act, yes, but one worthy of Rahab later being listed as a hero of the faith? Apparently this wasn't the last to be heard of Rahab. This act did save her life, but her change of heart as she sought the Lord saved her soul. She is called "righteous" in James 2:25, and Matthew 1:5 lists her in the genealogy of Christ. We must assume she put aside her former "profession" and turned to follow God.

Perhaps you think yourself without virtue. It may be that you haven't always been the best example or have portions of your life of which you're not particularly proud. You may question, "How can I be an example of virtue to my children when I've been such a failure in so many ways?"

Rahab would certainly be considered a moral failure in today's society—no one we would hold up as an example of virtue. However, she changed her heart and changed her ways. And she gained exceptional honor because of it, forever remembered for faith.

What about you? Are you ready to make some changes?

Gracious Father,
we both know the sins of my past.
Forgive me and restore me.
Let others see the change in me
and grow in faith as well.

THE MARK OF A MOTHER

Children are the living messages
we send to a time we will not see.
—John Whitehead[120]

Follow my example, as I follow the example of Christ.
1 Corinthians 11:1

O say! Can you see, by the dawn's early light? . . ." These words from the *Star-Spangled Banner* are often sung with great pride and emotion as we behold our nation's flag—the banner that represents our country. Every schoolchild learns that the thirteen stripes stand for the original thirteen colonies and that the fifty stars represent the fifty states in the Union. When a flag is burned, we are outraged as this is a sign of rebellion or hatred against the country we love. The flag symbolizes the best in patriotism and honor.

We are a society that loves its symbols and logos. We can tell if a person is married by looking at his or her left hand for a ring—the symbol of marriage. The tiniest toddler can find a fast-food restaurant within minutes. She knows behind the symbol of those golden arches she'll find a Happy Meal with a prize inside. We know which sports teams a person roots for by the colors of his clothes on a game day. Recent ads for Nike haven't even shown an athletic shoe or a slogan. Instead we look at a picture of Michael Jordan slamming a basketball, see a miniscule Nike "swoosh" in the corner of the page, and know what we're supposed to buy. Children pick up cigarettes because Joe Camel is cool. An illiterate person can drive in America because we use symbols on our road signs. We even remember Christ through the symbol of a cross. The list goes on and on!

We are often remembered through symbols as well. Author John Trent says, "When I think of my childhood, my thoughts stumble upon a thousand pictures of my mother's hands." His mother had severe rheumatoid arthritis, so any time she used her twisted hands, it was gently and with love. These hands are the symbol of her love.[121]

Our own mother could be symbolized by a loaf of homemade bread. She grinds the wheat herself and gives this delicious and light bread as gifts. It is a symbol to us of her compassion and hospitality—she loves to bring hungry and lonely people into her home and feed them. She loves to prepare and deliver a meal for someone just out of the hospital. She cannot let you into her home without feeding you, caring for you, and putting her arms around you.

Our sister Jill could be symbolized by a rose. Classy. Rich in color. She is strong enough to stand up to the rough rains, yet soft to the touch. And as the fragrance of a rose fills a room, so does Jill's wonderful laughter.

Our sister Annette is characterized by her middle

name, Joy. She brings laughter and happiness to everyone she encounters. When others are stressed about traffic, bills, war, and any other problem of life, Annette will smile and offer a hug. Her mind cannot understand many of the complexities of life, so she helps others find joy in the simple things in life.

Now what about you? What symbols will you be known by? You might laugh as you think of being remembered for your car keys since you spent so much time chauffeuring kids around, or joke about being remembered with a lump of charcoal for all the times you burned dinner. But seriously, we will all be remembered for something. What will it be?

Throughout this book we've discussed numerous virtues, all of which are important. These are the symbols by which we can be remembered. Will your children remember the compassion of your heart? The humility of your spirit? Your forgiving nature? The joy with which you embraced life? The courage with which you faced adversity? The purity of your actions? Your unflagging faith in God?

We pass our legacy on to our children. Leave them virtue.

God, let the virtues of our hearts
be known through our words and actions.
Let us be remembered as women of virtue.

NOTES

1. As quoted by John Maxwell in "What Children Owe Their Parents (and Themselves)," *Preaching Today*, Tape No. 140.
2. "Father's Eyes," written by Gary Chapman, recorded by Amy Grant on *My Father's Eyes*, Myrrh, 1979.
3. *The American Heritage Dictionary of the English Language*, Third Edition, Houghton Mifflin, 1996, electronic version.
4. As quoted in *Women of Character*, edited by Lawrence Kimbrough, Broadman & Holman Publishing, 1998, page 15.
5. As quoted by Jackie Gleason in *Laffirmations: 1,001 Ways to Add Humor to Your Life and Work* by Joel Goodman, Health Communications, Inc., Deerfield Beach, FL, 1995, page 57.
6. From "A Home for Rosie," *Family Circle,* May 12, 1998, page 100.
7. "Down in My Heart," by George W. Cooke, Word Music/ASCAP, 1977.
8. As quoted in *Choosing to Live the Blessing*, by John Trent, WaterBrook Press, 1997, page 195.
9. As quoted in *Kids Say the Cutest Things About Moms*, compiled by Dandi Daley Mackall, Trade Life Books, Inc., 1997, page 14.
10. As portrayed by Ed Gwynn, *Mary Poppins,* Walt Disney, 1964.
11. *Christian Single*, March 1997, page 31.
12. As quoted in "Quotable Quotes," *Reader's Digest*, January 1998, page 185.
13. "Discipline" in *The Complete Book of Sensible Sayings and Wacky Wit* by Vern McLellan, Tyndale House Publishers, Wheaton, IL, 1998, page 75.
14. From *Tidbits of Loveland, Berthoud, and Estes Park,* Vol 3, Issue 45.
15. "The Question is Why?" *Sports Illustrated,* November 2, 1998, page 60.
16. "Restraint" in *Growing Strong in the Seasons of Life,* by Charles R. Swindoll, Zondervan Publishing House, 1983, page 408.
17. From *The Complete Live and Learn and Pass it On*, edited by H. Jackson Brown, Rutledge Hill Press, 1998, page 177.
18. As portrayed by Julie Andrews, "A Spoonful of Sugar," by Richard and Robert Sherman, *Mary Poppins*, Walt Disney.
19. "Stuck on Bubble Gum," by Susan B. McGrath, *National Geographic World*, September 1998, pages 22-24. And "Bubble Gum Science", by the editors of *Klutz,* Klutz Press, 1997.
20. Quoted in *The Complete Book of Sensible Sayings & Wacky Wit,* by Vern McLellan, Tyndale House Publishers, Wheaton, IL, 1998, p. 32.
21. "Say what?" *The Denver Post,* September 28, 1998, 2F.
22. *Webster's Ninth New Collegiate Dictionary,* Merriam-Webster, 1986.
23. As quoted in *The Winner Within* by Pat Riley, G.P. Putnam's Sons, 1993, page 80.

24. "Wild and Wacky Inventions" from the instructional pamphlet, *Super Dooper Bouncing Zooom Balls* by Curiosity Kits, 1998.

25. "Whistle While You Work," *Snow White and the Seven Dwarfs*, Walt Disney Company.

26. "It's Laura's Fault," written by Phil Vischer and Kurt Heinecke, from *Big Idea's VeggieTunes 2*, Everland Entertainment/Word Distribution, 1998.

27. Some of these are from our own homes, others are listed on the web site, "Stupid Product Warnings and Instructions."

28. "Friend of a Wounded Heart" by Wayne Watson and Clair Cloninger, Word Music, 1987.

29. "You Take Care of Your Family" by Judi Dash, *Family Circle Magazine,* May 12, 1998, page 96.

30. As quoted in *The Complete Book of Sensible Sayings & Wacky Wit,* by Vern McLellan, Tyndale House Publishers, Wheaton, IL, 1998, page 229.

31. From *Tidbits* newsletter. John A. Skradski, Publisher. Loveland, Berthoud, and Estes Park, October 1, 1998.

32. "Stand" by Phil Vischer and Kurt Heinecke, *Big Idea's VeggieTunes 2*, Everland Entertainment/Word Distribution, 1998.

33. "Heroes for Today," *Reader's Digest*, October 1998, page 56.

34. *The Book of Unusual Quotations*, edited by Rudolf Flesch, Harper & Brothers, New York, NY, page 208.

35. "Research Won't Let Sleeping Bears Lie," Mark Eddy, *The Denver Post*, September 6, 1998; A1.

36. *Adam Bede*, chapter 42, 1859, *The Columbia Dictionary of Quotations*, Columbia University Press, 1993.

37. "Searching for a Home," *Reporter-Herald*, September 23, 1998, page A-10.

38. "Heartbeat of Heaven," recorded by Steven Curtis Chapman, on *Heaven in the Real World.* Sparrow Song/Peach Hill Songs (BMI), 1994 .

39. "Seconds, Anyone?" by Samantha Miller, *People Magazine*, September 1, 1997, page 94.

40. *Winnie the Pooh*, by A. A. Milne, Dell Publishing, 1926.

41. "I Will Be Your Friend," written by Michelle Lewis, Dane Devillier, and Sean Hosein. Recorded by Amy Grant on *Behind the Eyes,* Careers-BMG Music Publishing, Inc, 1997.

42. "Virtue in Action: Woman of Virtue," *Virtue*, January/February 1998, page 16.

43. "Fresh Start," *People*, August 10, 1998, page 52.

44. AskJeeves.com/MotherTeresa/quotes

45. *Mother Teresa: Protector of the Sick* by Linda Carlson Johnson, Blackbirch Press, 1991.

46. From "Gems From a Thousand Sources" by F. H. (Rick) Ricketson, Jr., Monitor

Publications, Inc., Denver, CO, page 80.

47. As noted on www.funytown.com

48. "Generosity" in *The Complete Book of Sensible Sayings & Wacky Wit* by Vern McLellan, Tyndale House Publishers, Wheaton, IL, 1998, page 108.

49. "Employer Takes Hostage's Place" by David Crary, *The Denver Post*, November 7, 1998.

50. As quoted in *Joined at the Heart: A Celebration of Friendship*, edited by Caroline Brownlow, Brownlow Publishing, 1998.

51. Ibid.

52. "The Three Little Pigs," by Paul Galdone, Houghton Mifflin/Clarion Books, 1970, New York.

53. "Quotable Quotes," *Reader's Digest*, January 1997, page 161.

54. From the 1998 *Mary Englebreit Desk Calendar*, Wednesday, October 7.

55. From the 1998 *Mary Englebreit Desk Calendar*, Tuesday, October 20.

56. "That's What Friends Are For," written by Richard and Robert Sherman, from *The Jungle Book*, Walt Disney, 1964.

57. From the 1998 *Mary Englebreit Desk Calendar*, Monday, November 2.

58. "Always Sisters," by CeCe, Angie, and Debbie Winans, *Sisters: The Story Goes On*, Warner Alliance, 1995.

59. *Letters from New York*, Vol. 1, Letter 26, 1843.

60. *The Language of Flowers*, by Margaret Pickston, Michael Joseph Ltd., 1968.

61. *The Topical Encyclopedia of Living Quotations*, edited by Sherwood Eliot Wirt and Kersten Beckstrom, Bethany House Publishers, 1982.

62. "Finding Forgiveness," by Missy Jenkins, as told to Kay Lawing Gupton, *Today's Christian Woman,* September/October 1998, page 74.

63. As quoted in *The Columbia Dictionary of Quotations*, Columbia University Press, 1993.

64. "I Can't Believe I Did That!" *Parents* magazine, compiled by Eva Pomice, September 1998, page 29.

65. "I'll Be There for You" by the Rembrandts, for the television show *Friends.* Atlantic Recording Group.

66. "UNC's Dalton Takes One for the Team" by Dylan B. Tomlinson, *The Denver Post,* Friday, November 20, 1998, page 10D.

67. From "Gems From a Thousand Sources," by F. H. (Rick) Rickertson, Jr., Monitor Publications, Inc., Denver, CO, page 153.

68. *Good Dog, Carl,* by Alexandra Day, Simon & Schuster Books for Young Readers, 1985.

69. As quoted in *Women of Character*, edited by Lawrence Kimbrough, Broadman & Holman Publishers, 1998, page 79.

70. *Love You Forever,* by Robert Munsch, Firefly Books, 1986.

71. *The Little Prince*, by Antoine de Saint-Exupéry, Harcourt Brace & Company, 1943.
72. From the files of *Leadership*, *Bible Illustrator 3*, Parsons Technology.
73. "This Is What Love Is," by John Elefante, *Windows of Heaven*, Word Records, 1995.
74. In *Evil Hour* (1968) from *Microsoft Bookshelf 98*.
75. From "Gems From a Thousand Sources" by F. H. (Rick) Ricketson, Jr., Monitor Publications, Denver, CO, page 54.
76. "Who Speaks for the Victims," Paula Spencer, *Woman's Day,* June 2, 1998, page 57.
77. "Giving Voice to the Innocent," Paula Spencer, *Woman's Day*, June 2, 1998, page 60.
78. Ibid.
79. "Making Sure Justice Is Done," Suzanne Leigh, *Family Circle,* May 12, 1998, page 13.
80. "This Girl Gets Her Kicks," by Rick Reilly, *Sports Illustrated*, October 19, 1998, page 100.
81. "Here's the Kicker: Queen's Crowing Achievement Is on the Field," Bill Konigsberg, *The Denver Post*, October 9, 1998, 10D.
82. As portrayed by Frank Morgan in *The Wizard of Oz*, MGM/UA Home Video, 1939.
83. *The Voyage of the Dawn Treader*, by C. S. Lewis, The Macmillan Company, 1952, page 160.
84. "Seven from Heaven," by Bonnie Shepherd, *Focus on the Family*, November 1998, pages10-13.
85. *The Authoritative Calvin and Hobbes: A Calvin and Hobbes Treasury,* Bill Watterson, Universal Press Syndicate, 1990, page 36.
86. Found at http://instruct.unc.edu
87. As portrayed by Olympia Dukakis in *Steel Magnolias*, 1989, Tri-Star Pictures, Inc.
88. *Webster's Ninth New Collegiate Dictionary,* Merriam-Webster Inc., 1985, page 299.
89. "Learning Experience for All," Chris Kahn, *The Arizona Republic*, September 16, 1998, page B1.
90. *Tidbits of Loveland, Berthoud, and Estes Park*, Vol. 3, Issue 45.
91. "Honesty in America," *Family Circle,* June 2, 1998, page 48.
92. *Leadership*, Vol. 16, no. 4.
93. *Just Like Jesus,* by Max Lucado, Word Publishing, Nashville, TN, 1998, page 112.
94. Ibid.

95. As portrayed by Bernadette Peters in *Rodgers & Hammerstein's Cinderella*, Walt Disney, 1998.

96. As quoted in *How to Be a Happy Parent. . .In Spite of Your Children*, ch. 11, 1995.

97. " 'Shortcut' Gets Driver in a Bunch of Trouble" by the Associated Press, *The Denver Post,* September 17, 1998, B2.

98. "Work," *Women Talk*, edited by Michelle Brown and Ann O'Connor, 1984, as quoted in *The Columbia Dictionary of Quotations,* Columbia University Press, 1993.

99. *Polish Your Furniture with Panty Hose* by Joey Green, Hyperion, 1995.

100. "Old Enough to Know" written by Michael W. Smith and Wayne Kirkpatrick. *The First Decade,* O-Ryan Music, Inc. (ASCAP)/Careers-BMG Music Publishing, Inc. (BMI), 1985.

101. "Breaking the Cycle," by Kathleen Howley, in *American Enterprise.* Included in "Heroes for Today" in *Reader's Digest,* July 1998, page 84.

102. "Wait a Little Longer" by Wayne Watson, *Field of Souls,* 1995, Material Music/Word ASCAP.

103. "Smallpox," *Microsoft Encarta 96 Encyclopedia*, 1993-1995, Microsoft Corporation.

104. "Virus," *Microsoft Encarta 96 Encyclopedia*, 1993-1995, Microsoft Corporation.

105. *The Second Coming of the Church,* George Barna, Word Publishing, 1998.

106. "Stats and Studies," *Children's Ministry Magazine,* November/December 1998, page 12.

107. *Best From the Farmers' Almanac,* edited by Ray Geiger, Doubleday & Company, Inc., 1963.

108. "The Ringling Bros. and Barnum & Bailey Program of Displays" presented by Feld Entertainment, 1998, Feld Entertainment, Inc.

109. "Love Song for a Savior," written by Dan Haseltine, *Jars of Clay*, Brentwood Music.

110. "The Wind Beneath My Wings," written by Larry Henley and Jeff Silbar, as performed on the *Beaches Soundtrack*.

111. *Science and the Bible*, by Donald B. DeYoung, Baker Books, 1994, pages 52-54.

112. "How Great Thou Art," written by Stuart K. Hine, *Hymns for the Family of God,* Paragon Association, Nashville, TN, 1976, page 2.

113. *Nature Is Stranger Than Fiction,* John Y. Beaty, as excerpted in *Best From the Farmers' Almanac*, edited by Ray Geiger, Doubleday & Company, Inc., Garden City, NY, 1963, 95.

114. "Blowin' in the Wind," written by Bob Dylan, 1962.

115. "The Beauty of the Cross" written by Brian Ray, recorded by Crystal Lewis on *Beauty for Ashes*, 1996, Metro One/ASCAP.

116. *Peace of Mind Is a Blanket That Purrs*, by Pat Brady, Rutledge Hill Press, 1998.

117. "For Who He Really Is," written by Steven Curtis Chapman and Geoff Moore, on *Real Life Conversations,* 1988, Sparrow Song/New Wings Music.

118. "Right Writers" *The Denver Post*, September 22, 1998, 2E.

119. "Wild Imagination," written by Kyle Matthews, recorded by Scott Krippayne on *Wild Imagination*, Word Records, 1995.

120. As quoted in *Women of Character*, edited by Lawrence Kimbrough, Broadman & Holman Publishing, 1998, page 123.

121. *Choosing to Live the Blessing*, by John Trent, WaterBrook Press, 1997, page 126.

It's Been An Affair to Remember

Great Inspirational Songs from the Matriarch of Gospel's Most Renowned Dynasty

After giving birth to some of the gospel world's brightest names such as CeCe Winans, BeBe Winans, the Winans, Angie & Debbie Winans and others, Delores "Mom" Winans is giving birth to her own ministry with her very first solo album. "It's Been An Affair To Remember" celebrates Mom's life-long "affair" with God and the blessings that He has sent her way.

Backed by the world-renowned London Symphony Orchestra, Mom's smooth alto graces such church standards as "I Must Tell Jesus," "Tis So Sweet/Trust and Obey," "His Eye Is On The Sparrow," "Kum Ba Ya, "I'll Give You Jesus," "Sweet Hour of Prayer," "Ordinary People" and the title cut which was composed by her daughter Angie.

Produced by the Grammy-winning duo of Cedric & Victor Caldwell for Caldwell Plus Productions.
Available in stores everywhere. Also available via our website at www.againsttheflowrecords.com
For media and other information on Mom Winans, visit our publicity firm Capital Entertainment's website at www.capitalentertainment.com